CHILDREN ACT 1989

A Report by the Secretaries of State for Health and for Wales on the Children Act 1989 in pursuance of their duties under Section 83(6) of the Act.

n 2144   LONDON: HMSO   £15.85 net

Table of Contents

Preface

This is the first report to Parliament on the working of the Children Act 1989. Considerable claims have been made for this Act. If this is not just empty rhetoric, however, tangible gains which have appeared during the year must be identified. We are pleased to say it is possible to do this.

This report contains a comprehensive description of the operations and achievements of the Act. One of the most striking and encouraging features of 1992 has been the way in which local authority interventions have become more sharply focused, with more children remaining with their own families.

Although the trends have not stabilised, in the first year almost 3,000 or broadly 50 per cent fewer emergency orders were made giving authority for the removal of a child from home. The reduction in these orders suggests that local authorities are being more discriminating than previously and are using the power of emergency intervention more appropriately.

There has been a substantial fall in the number of children entering compulsory care. Some 1,600 were subject to a care order under the Children Act in the first year compared with nearly 4 times as many under similar orders previously. This is a strong indication that the culture of a working partnership with parents is becoming a reality in the vast majority of authorities.

Some 5,000 or 10 per cent fewer children were being 'looked after' by local authorities at the end of March compared with a year before. This was what the Act intended. In general, the best place for children to grow up is in their own homes with their own families. This aim of the Act is being achieved with authorities working together with families to provide help to keep the family together.

These solid achievements could not have been secured without the enthusiasm, commitment and interest which the Act inspired country-wide in professionals and non-professionals alike. We are confident that further progress on this and other fronts will be made during 1993.

Virginia Bottomley

Secretary of State for Health

Secretary of State for Wales

February 1993

PART I

Chapter 1: Introduction

Background

1.1   This is the first report by the Secretaries of State for Health and for Wales on the Children Act 1989. The Act received its Royal Assent on 16 November 1989 and was implemented on 14 October 1991. The period covered by the report is the first year of the Children Act in operation.

1.2   Under Section 83(6) the Secretary of State is required to lay before Parliament each year a consolidated and classified abstract of information in respect of local authority functions relating to children, certain services for children provided by voluntary organisations and court proceedings under the Act. There will be a further response under section 83(6) later in 1993 which will draw on the regular statistical sources and provide the first in the statistical abstracts reporting the position after the Act was implemented.

1.3   In so short a timescale it is difficult to gauge the success or otherwise of such an important piece of legislation. There are, however, some encouraging trends to report as well as some early difficulties. What the report seeks to achieve is a broad view of progress towards implementation of the Act nationwide. The focus of the report is therefore wideranging and encompasses a variety of child care themes including:

- progress in implementing the provisions concerning residential care.
- child protection cases and cases of children looked after by local authorities which remain unallocated to social workers. This is a further response to the second report from the Health Select Committee (1990–91) on Child Protection Services.
- the adequacy of child care training generally in compliance with the Secretary of State's review duty under S 83(8) of the Children Act.

1.4   Throughout the report, the word 'children' is used to describe children and young persons under the age of 18.

Principles and Philosophy of the Act

1.5   The legislative framework for the provision of services to children was altered radically by the Act. Its provisions are far reaching and affect most aspects of services for children and adolescents and their families as well as having a major impact on the courts, the police, education services, the health service, children's voluntary organisations and the private child care sector.

1.6   The Act is a charter for children. Its overriding purpose is to promote and protect children's welfare and in so doing it draws together and simplifies previous legislation to produce a practical and consistent code.

1.7   The Act brings together for the first time the public and private law relating to children. It seeks to strike a balance between the rights of children to express their views on decisions made about their lives, the rights of parents to exercise their responsibilities towards the child and the duty of the state to intervene where the child's welfare requires it.

1.8   Central to the philosophy of the Act is the belief that children are best looked after within the family with both parents playing a full part and without resort to legal proceedings. This is reflected in the new concept of 'parental responsibility'. Parents retain parental responsibility when they separate following private law proceedings and continue to do so when their child is looked after by the local authority. Parental responsibility is only lost when a child is freed for adoption or adopted. Unmarried fathers may obtain parental responsibility by agreement with the mother or through court orders.

1.9   Local authorities now have duties to promote the upbringing of children in need by their families so far as is consistent with their welfare. To meet these local authorities are required to identify children in need in their area and provide a range and level of support services. Racial origin, culture and linguistic background are factors authorities must take into account when making plans for children. They also have a duty to promote contact between children whom they are looking after and their families.

1.10   The Act contains a new, simplified legal framework for the care and protection of children and introduces new orders for use when children are at risk of significant harm. Care and supervision orders are retained but there is now only one route by which the courts can make such orders. The new education supervision order enables local education authorities to take action where children are not receiving a proper education.

1.11   Under the Act, local authorities have new duties to ensure that the welfare of children being looked after away from home is properly safeguarded as regards their health, education and general quality of life. It also ensures that facilities such as nurseries and playgroups (including out-of-school facilities for children upto age eight) and people such as childminders are safeguarding the welfare of children in their care.

1.12   The Children Act gives parents improved rights, including the right to a say in the plans being made for their child's future and maintains their right to attend and be represented at any court proceedings under the Act involving their child.

1.13   The child's voice too, must be heard when decisions about their future are being taken. In contested private law proceedings and in applications for care and supervision orders the court must consider a checklist of factors, focusing particularly on the needs of the child but also on his or her own views and wishes and on the options available to the court before coming to a decision. This requirement to pay attention to the wishes and feelings of the child has been given added impetus by the United Nations Convention on the Rights of the Child. The Children Act meets the obligations in whole or in part of many of the main articles in the Convention, which was ratified by the UK Government in December 1991.

1.14   The Act, while requiring any compulsory intervention in a child's life to be authorised by a court, seeks to discourage unnecessary court intervention in family life by prohibiting the making of any order unless it will positively benefit the child. The Act also makes explicit, for the first time, that delay is generally harmful to children and should be avoided.

1.15   To translate these principles into practice has required not only a major shift in approach to the provision of services by child care professionals but has manifest itself in changes to the structure of service delivery, most notably in the courts hearing children's cases.

Court Structure

1.16   The Children Act establishes for the first time a concurrent jurisdiction covering magistrates' (family proceedings) courts, county courts and the High Court so that children's cases are heard at the appropriate level of court by specially trained and experienced judiciary and together with other related proceedings wherever appropriate.

1.17   By enabling the transfer of cases both laterally (eg between family proceedings courts) and vertically (eg from family proceedings court to county court) the system is designed to provide a flexible framework to ensure that cases are heard swiftly and by the appropriate tier of court. Two principles that apply to the transfer of **any** case are that the transfer must be:

- in the best interests of the child
- delay must be avoided if it is likely to prejudice the welfare of the child.

1.18   Monitoring the operation of the Children Act in the courts has been undertaken by the Home Office and Lord Chancellor's Department through the collection of statistics. A countrywide network of committees which report back to the Children Act Advisory Committee has also been created. The central committee, under the chairmanship of Mrs Justice Booth, reports to the Lord Chancellor, the Home Secretary, the Secretary of State for Health and the President of the Family Division. It presented its first annual report on 17 November 1992.

Implementation Programme

1.19   It was recognised at a very early stage that preparing front line practitioners, their supervisors and managers across a wide range of child care disciplines for the changes heralded by the Act would involve extensive training and implementation programmes.

1.20   The Department of Health and the Social Services Inspectorate (SSI) convened the Joint Action for Implementation Group (JAFIG) to oversee a multi-agency programme of work leading up to implementation of the Act. Members of JAFIG included representatives from other Government Departments, the Local Authority Associations, the Association of Directors of Social Services (ADSS), the Central Council for Education and Training in Social Work (CCETSW), the National Council for Voluntary Child Care Organisations (NCVCCO) and the Law Society.

1.21   In Wales a similar steering group was established and Social Information Systems Ltd was contracted by the steering group, with Welsh Office financial support, to give assistance to each local authority in its planning for the Act. That approach was highly successful. One of its effects was to produce a degree of consistency in the general planning approach adopted by all 8 authorities which considerably facilitated the subsequent implementation planning agenda. The Social Services Inspectorate, Wales, ran a number of inter-authority, inter-agency workshops on the implementation of the Act. One series of seminars dealt with developing services for children in need; another addressed the court and legal processors. A great deal of other planning and development work took place in Wales, organised by the local authorities themselves and by almost every significant child care agency working in the Principality. In addition, a Circular on Inter-Agency collaboration was issued on 30 August 1991. It laid stress on the need for all relevant authorities, including housing authorities, to collaborate in the development of services under Part III of the Act. The Circular called for progress reports to be submitted by 31 December 1992.

1.22   In an unprecedented exercise to inform and disseminate widely, the Department of Health and Welsh Office spent over £2m promulgating ten volumes of guidance and Regulations on the Children Act—including a recently completed index to the series—a revised version of 'Working Together' and commissioning a number of training projects for use by local authorities and voluntary organisations. A series of practice guides were similarly disseminated to accompany some of the volumes of Guidance and Regulations, as was 'Patterns and Outcomes in Child Placement', a review of current child care research. The training projects were aimed at promoting inter-disciplinary training at both basic awareness and specialist levels. Copies of the training packs were also made available to local authorities and key child care voluntary organisations through the NCVCCO.

1.23   An introductory guide and training materials for the NHS were produced to assist staff working in the health sector to understand those provisions of the Act which are likely to be of most interest and relevance to them. A further £250,000 was spent on the Judicial Studies Board training programme for judges and magistrates. The Government's Training Support Programme, which is targeted at the training needs of particular groups of local authority staff, earmarked £2.5m in 1990/91 specifically for Children Act training, with a further £3m in 1991/92.

1.24   To raise the general level of awareness of the Act's provisions amongst the public, the Department commissioned the production of a video and adviser's guide for use by local support groups and published a range of booklets for parents. These explain parents' rights and responsibilities in relation to their children in the court setting and in their dealings with local authority social services departments. A further booklet was prepared on the Act's day care provisions and the new review duty.

1.25   To help children and young people to express their views effectively and to exercise their rights under the Act, the Department produced a 'first steps' leaflet followed by a series of booklets explaining in straightforward language what the Act meant for them. The leaflet and booklets were distributed free of charge to Citizens Advice Bureaux, libraries and other advice centres. The Lord Chancellor's Department bought copies for placement in all care and family hearing centres. Around 1.5 million leaflets were inserted in one edition of three youth magazines. Sufficient copies of the booklets were sent to each Director of Social Services to allow for their distribution to every child of sufficient understanding who was being looked after by the authority. In the financial year 1991/92 £725,000 was spent on publicising the Children Act. (A complete list of government guidance, sponsored training and information packs in relation to the Act is appended at Annex C).

1.26   This comprehensive dissemination exercise mounted by the Department of Health involved detailed consultation and discussion with other Government departments, the Local Authority Associations, voluntary organisations and consumer interests. It is encouraging that this breadth of dialogue has continued throughout the early months of the Act in operation, paving the way for future work, including the assessments and developments arising from implementation.

1.27   As an example of this continuing programme the Department of Health sponsored a project under the leadership of Professor Roy Parker at the University of Bristol in regard to children looked after by a local authority. The project, 'Looking After Children: Assessing Outcomes in Child Care' has provided a series of assessment and action records or schedules to measure the progress and development of children 'looked after'. These schedules guide social workers and others to pay regard to important aspects of health and educational progress and a range of other practical issues which can be missed or under-rated when children are in care. Other aspects of social development and behaviour are also recorded. The schedules have been designed to reflect the requirements of the respective Children Act Regulations.

1.28   Sponsored by SSI and assisted by the National Children's Bureau (NCB) the university staff have introduced their schedules and their application to groups of senior SSD managers and practitioners at a series of regional seminars. The methods for assessment and review, conducted in partnership with parents and in consultation with children, as the Act requires, have been piloted in sample authorities. All the indications so far are that this is an outstanding action-based research project which assists greatly in implementing the Act in a very practical manner.

Monitoring Strategy

1.29   The Department of Health's strategy to monitor implementation of the Children Act was launched in February 1992. It recognised that the process would span several years and involve assessing changes to services and the views of those who receive them.

1.30   The strategy set about identifying the existing mechanisms by which progress in implementing the Act could be measured and by developing requirements in the longer term to enable any gaps in the Government's sources of information to be filled. It is these sources of management information that will form the basis of this and future reports.

1.31   Timely and accurate management information returns are a pre-requisite for effective monitoring. The Department has improved its statistical collections to take account of the changes introduced by the Children Act. Returns from local authorities covering the first six months of the Act were completed at 31 March 1992. The first full year's returns will be completed a year later.

1.32   The most extensive return is the new 'Children looked after' return. A separate return is made for each child in care, accommodated voluntarily under section 20 of the Act or accommodated compulsorily by the local authority. The new returns will link from one year to another so as to chart care histories. For the first time information on the continuous period a child has been looked after is being collected, and placement information is collected on a continuous basis throughout the year rather than as a snapshot. The day care and child protection returns have also been expanded.

1.33   The Department, in discussion with the local authorities, is currently considering a new return on services provided to children in need and their families and adding ethnic origin information to particular children's services statistics. There are also plans to introduce a new statistical return covering adoption to supplement existing incomplete data on the subject.

The National Monitoring Survey

1.34   In the knowledge that accurate and comprehensive management information could not be available in time for this first report to Parliament, the Department of Health, through the Social Services Inspectorate, initiated a major national survey of all 108 local authorities in England. Local authorities in Wales received a scaled down version of the survey to complement information already available from other sources.

1.35   The purpose of the survey was to elicit the extent to which particular Children Act provisions have been implemented and their impact on child care services and any development of policy arising from implementation. The need to extract quantifiable information that would signal early pressure points in the progress towards implementation determined both the areas of the Act for consideration and the breadth of questions posed. The subject areas selected were as follows:

- ● Residential Care

- ● Private Homes and Independent Schools

- ● Daycare and Review Duty

- ● Representations and Complaints

- ● Publishing Information on Available Services

- ● Children with Disabilities

1.36   In addition, local authorities were asked to report back information on unallocated casework and on progress in implementing 'Working Together'. Questions were also asked to determine the extent of change in the structure of service delivery flowing from the requirements of the Community Care legislation and which may have had consequences for children's services.

1.37   Recognising the burden such survey exercises place on local authorities, the timing of this one was chosen with some care so as not to coincide with similar monitoring exercises on the community care front. It is, however, indicative of the breadth of support and enthusiasm engendered by this Act that so many local authorities in England and Wales were willing to co-operate in the survey. Although not all local authorities completed all parts of the questionnaire, every local authority in England and Wales submitted some form of response. Where the findings in the report rely on less than a 100% response rate this is indicated in the text and accompanying tables.

1.38   Local authorities were asked to complete the survey as at 30 June 1992 thereby enabling observations to be made covering the first nine months of the Act in operation. In interpreting the findings, the date of the survey needs to be borne in mind. Local authorities have continued to forge ahead with implementation of the Act and it is known that further progress was made between June and October 1992 in achieving targets right across the board.

1.39   Three other surveys undertaken during 1991/92, all of which have contributed information to this report, complemented the national survey. These are:

(i)   Capitalising on the Act—A Working Party Report on the Implementation of the Children Act in London. The Working Party was set up as a joint initiative by the Social Services Inspectorate (London Region), the National Council for Voluntary Child Care Organisations, the Association of Directors of Social Services, the Panels of Guardians *ad litem* in London and the London Borough Regional Children's Planning Committee. The Report describes a monitoring exercise conducted across London which aimed at providing a picture of progress in implementing key areas of the Act after the first six months. It suggests that an effect of the Act has been to protect children's services budgets, relative to other client groups.

(ii)   First Key, the National Leaving Care Advisory Service, with Departmental support, initiated a monitoring exercise, which sought to collect information on developments in the field of leaving care/after care work with young people. A questionnaire was circulated to all local authorities in England and Wales. Authorities were also asked to provide copies of local policy statements and information leaflets. A summary report was published on 30 November 1992. Further work is now in hand to analyse the more detailed policy statements.

(iii) As part of the Department's child care research programme Dr Jane Aldgate of the Department of Applied Social Studies and Social Research at Oxford University and Ms Jane Tunstill of the National Council for Voluntary Child Care Organisations were commissioned to explore ways in which local authorities are implementing section 17 of the Children Act in relation to children in need. Integral to that research, was a comprehensive survey questionnaire, again circulated to all local authorities in England.

Research

1.40   The Department has consistently recognised the value of research in contributing to both policy formulation and evaluation. As part of its' on-going child care research programme 12 new research projects have been commissioned specifically to monitor aspects of the Children Act. Broadly these cover court based intervention in child protection, the provision of family support services, day care and out of schools services, leaving care, residential care and children looked after generally. A portfolio of relevant Department of Health funded research abstracts and their likely completion dates appears at Annex A.

Social Services Inspectorate Role

1.41   A final, but essential, strand in the Department's monitoring strategy is the role played by Social Services Inspectorate. SSI is a professional division of the Department of Health, headed by the Chief Inspector. He is responsible to the Secretary of State for professional advice on Government policy and on the quality of social services provision. SSI is independent of local authority, voluntary and private social services agencies.

1.42   In respect of the Children Act, SSI conducts a rolling programme under the Secretary of State's powers to inspect voluntary children's homes and local authority secure accommodation for young persons. There is also a programme now underway to inspect particular aspects in relation to implementation of the Children Act. These will be conducted in representative samples of authorities in England. Additionally, SSI will conduct a number of studies not under inspectorial powers, to examine aspects of implementation where further concern is identified or the need for more information becomes apparent.

Resources

1.43   The additional resources needed by local authorities for implementation of the Act were considered in detail during discussions with the Local Authority Associations as part of the Public Expenditure Surveys in 1990 and 1991. For their part the Local Authority Associations trawled social services departments for a local view of resource needs.

1.44   Standard spending on personal social services in 1991/92 increased by 23 per cent over the previous year, providing among other services, for the part year costs of the Children Act. By 1992/93, the first full year of the Act, standard spending for children's services was up 27 per cent over that in 1990/91—a 14% increase in real terms over the two year period.

1.45   With the exception of a new specific grant, introduced from 1992/93 to target expenditure on the guardian *ad litem*service, and the contribution to child care training through the Training Support Grant, central Government financial support for local authorities is not hypothecated. It is for local authorities to allocate resources in accordance with local circumstances and priorities as well as legislative requirements.

Other Legislation

1.46   Finally, any assessment of local authority progress in implementing the Children Act needs to take account of a variety of factors that can be expected to have had an impact on performance. In particular, the scale of legislative change facing local authority social services departments in 1991/92 was considerable.

1.47   The community care changes enacted in the NHS and Community Care Act 1990, began to come into force in April 1991 with major implications for local authority social services, most sectors of the NHS, housing and the voluntary and private sector organisations concerned with services for adults. Planning for, and managing these changes has resulted in a substantial degree of re-organisation in the way local authorities deliver social services. Findings from the national survey suggest that 49 out of 90 local authorities experienced some form of organisational change across child care services during 1991 and 1992.

1.48   Additionally the Criminal Justice Act 1991, which came into effect in October 1992, has involved social services departments in preparation for the changes relating to their work with young offenders. The Act extends the remit of the juvenile court to embrace 17 year olds—renaming it the youth court. It requires social services to develop closer links and partnership with the probation service over matters such as producing pre-sentence reports and generally servicing the youth courts and places enhanced responsibilities on local authorities for children remanded to their accommodation. Additionally, the Act reforms the law on children's evidence, gives the court more flexible powers when dealing with 16 and 17 year olds in criminal proceedings and strengthens the courts' powers to involve parents or guardians (including, where relevant, the local authority) when children for whom they have parental responsibility offend.

PART II

Chapter 2: Child Protection and the Courts

Background

2.1   The new legal framework for compulsory intervention in the care and upbringing of children begins with the local authority's general duty to investigate children's circumstances whom they believe to be at risk of harm. Where that process of investigation requires the authority of a court order the Act ensures that such authority is given following proceedings in which the child, his parents and others with a legitimate concern for the child are able to participate fully. It is no longer possible for a local authority to assume parental rights to take a child into care or to restrict contact between a child and his family.

2.2   However, not all children's cases can or should come before the courts. Most child protection work is undertaken by local authority social services with the child remaining in the family home. This accords with the local authority's general duty to promote the upbringing of children in need by their families wherever possible and with the general presumption under the Act against making an order if it is possible to protect the child's welfare by other means.

2.3   In practice the decision about whether the assessed risk for a child is best managed on an entirely voluntary basis of work with families or requires the additional authority and framework of a court order will depend on a multiplicity of factors. These include the nature of the harm suffered or likely to be suffered, the surrounding circumstances, the parents' willingness to accept responsibility and to co-operate with the helping agencies and, where their care does not adequately meet the child's needs, an assessment of their ability to change.

2.4   Although the Children Act changes the available orders, venues, procedures and criteria, court remains a possible option for case management. The only justification for seeking a court order, however, is that the proposals for the child will in some definite and specific sense be an improvement on what might be achieved with a different order, or indeed, no order at all.

2.5   In many straight forward situations local authorities will continue to bring a range of non-court approaches to bear on work with families. Similarly, in the most serious of cases, the use of court proceedings, as before, will be inevitable.

2.6   Within this range exists a number of situations where a basic choice between court or non court routes still needs to be made, even though the local authority can demonstrate that the threshold criteria for the making of a care or emergency protection order apply. If the Children Act has succeeded in reducing public law applications, some shift in policy and practice must have taken place in the handling of these cases by local authorities.

2.7   Some measure of the extent to which the new approach of minimal court intervention and working in partnership has become embedded in practice can be gauged from an analysis of court workload activity in public law child care proceedings.

Court Activity

2.8   Statistics about the number of children subject to court proceedings in England and Wales between the implementation of the Act and 30 September 1992 are set out in tables 2.1–2.3.

● Table 2.1 shows the number of applications made and the outcome of completed cases for care and supervision and emergency protection orders, child assessment orders, education supervision orders and Section 34 contact orders.

● Table 2.2 and figure 2.1 show the number of applications and orders made in care, supervision and emergency protection order proceedings, in the period from 14 October 1991 to 31 December 1991 and for each subsequent quarter.

● Table 2.3 shows the number of applications made and the outcome for completed cases for Section 8 orders (ie residence, contact, prohibited steps, and specific issue) in public law proceedings. These include instances where a local authority is the applicant for a prohibited steps or specific issue order and others where another applicant, usually a member of the extended family has made an application for a Section 8 order, for example a residence and contact order, alongside a public law application by the local authority. As expected the number of these orders exceeds the number of applications, because the courts are able to make such orders on their own initiative.

Figures 2.2–2.4 show the outcome for completed cases.

Levels of application

2.9   There were more than 3,700 applications for a care order in the period from 14 October 1991 to 30 September 1992; some 2,200 applications for an emergency protection order and some 800 for supervision orders. Far fewer applications were received for child assessment orders (105) and for education supervision orders (137).

2.10   Figure 2.1 shows that the number of applications for care orders has increased each quarter, with a large increase (approx 25%) between the December 1991 quarter and the March 1992 quarter and a further 20% increase between the June and September quarters. Applications for supervision orders and emergency protection orders also showed an increase in March 1992. They have levelled off since then, with a marked reduction in the next quarter and a small increase thereafter.

Outcomes of completed cases

2.11   Figures 2.2–2.4 show that for emergency protection, care and supervision orders, orders made account for by far the greater part of completed applications —nearly 90%. The "withdrawn" category ranks second. In respect of applications for care orders there were more orders of "no order", that is where the courts did not consider that the order would be in the best interest of the child, than there were refusals in which the courts did not consider that the threshold criteria for making the order had been demonstrated. For EPOs and supervision orders there were more refusals than orders of "no order".

2.12   The numbers of completed emergency protection and supervision orders have kept broadly in step with the number of applications. This is not so with care orders. Care order proceedings are considerably longer—of the order of 10–12 weeks and this time lag between application and completion can be expected to have had an impact on the proportion of applications processed during the period. It is also likely, given the number of Section 8 orders made, that courts are using the menu of private law Section 8 orders as a preferred alternative to making a care order.

2.13   By 30 September 1992 only 50% of care order applications received since 14 October 1991 had resulted in a withdrawn application, a care order being made, an order of "no order" or a refusal. (Some care order applications will have resulted in an order of a different kind being made—eg a Section 8 order or a supervision order. The statistics do not link the order made and the application in such cases. It is therefore not possible to judge how many applications are still outstanding). As figure 2.1 shows, the number of care orders increases rapidly in the March and June quarters and showed a further increase in the September quarter. Further increases seem likely before the number of orders levels out.

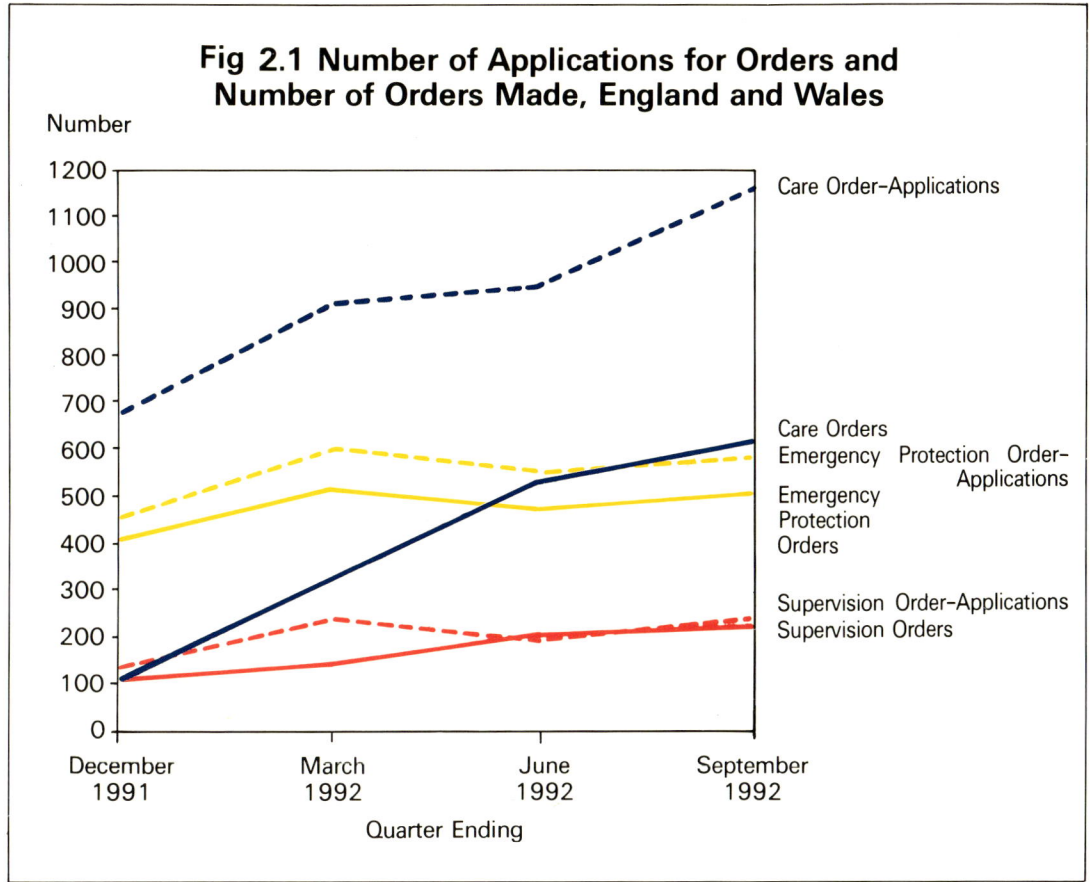

Fig 2.1 Number of Applications for Orders and Number of Orders Made, England and Wales

Comparisons with levels of activity before the Act

2.14   An expectation that the Children Act would result in lower levels of court activity appears to have been realised although in some cases exact comparison is not straightforward.

2.15   Making allowance for the fact the new statistics relate to slightly less than a full twelve months, by rounding up current figures the following comparisons emerge:

- 2,300 Emergency Protection Orders compared to about 5,000 children who were removed to a place of safety on the instructions of a magistrate in the year ending 31 March 1991.

- 600 children subject to supervision orders under the Children Act compared to some 2,500 subject to supervision order under the CYPA 1969 (excludes criminal supervision orders) and about the same number made in domestic matrimonial and wardship proceedings;

- 1,600 children subject to a care order under the Children Act compared to 3,300 subject to a full care order made under the CYPA 1969 (excluding criminal care orders) and about 2,900 children subject to a care order under other legislation (including interim orders) in the year ending 31 March 1991.

2.16   There are particular difficulties in comparing the situations before and after the Act was implemented in respect of care orders. Because of the time lag factors the number of care orders made in the twelve months since implementation is artificially low. Without this effect, the number of care orders made could have been expected to be between 2,500 and 3,000. Furthermore the nature of interim orders made in wardship and other proceedings before the Act was implemented was such that they could continue in force for many years. The figure 2,900 quoted above does generally include interim orders made in wardship and other domestic and matrimonial proceedings but may be an underestimate. Nonetheless, the numbers of children entering the care system through a court order are very much lower than in the comparable period immediately prior to implementation, and even allowing for time lag, "start up" effects this indicates a much lower level of court activity.

TABLE 2.1   Court Activity 14 October to 30 September 1992 (England and Wales)

Numbers of children

	Care Orders	Super-vision Orders	Emer-gency Protection Orders	Child Assess-ment Orders	Education Super-vision Orders	S34 Contact
Applications	3,715	841	2,215	105	137	1,460
Orders made	1,607	626	1,900	78	93	843
Orders of No Order	54	22	33	11	2	49
Applications Refused	28	26	88	4	1	86
Applications Withdrawn	167	50	141	30	6	120

Data for the September 1992 quarter are provisional.

TABLE 2.2   Applications and Orders by Calendar Quarter (England and Wales)

Numbers of children

		Quarter ending 31.12.91	Quarter ending 31.3.92	Quarter ending 30.6.92	Quarter ending 30.9.92
Care Orders	Applications	683	920	954	1,158
	Orders made	113	333	539	622
Supervision Orders	Applications	141	249	202	249
	Orders made	113	153	207	224
Emergency Protection Orders	Applications	465	604	561	585
	Orders made	407	523	467	503

Data for the September 1992 quarter are provisional.

TABLE 2.3   Section 8 Orders in Public Law Proceedings 14 October 1991 to 30 September 1992 (England and Wales)

Numbers of children

	Residence	Contact	Prohibited Steps	Specific Issue
Applications Made	520	284	373	48
Orders Made	1,016	643	662	125
Orders of No Order	40	24	10	4
Applications Refused	36	22	8	0
Applications Withdrawn	52	36	34	4

Data for the September 1992 quarter are provisional.

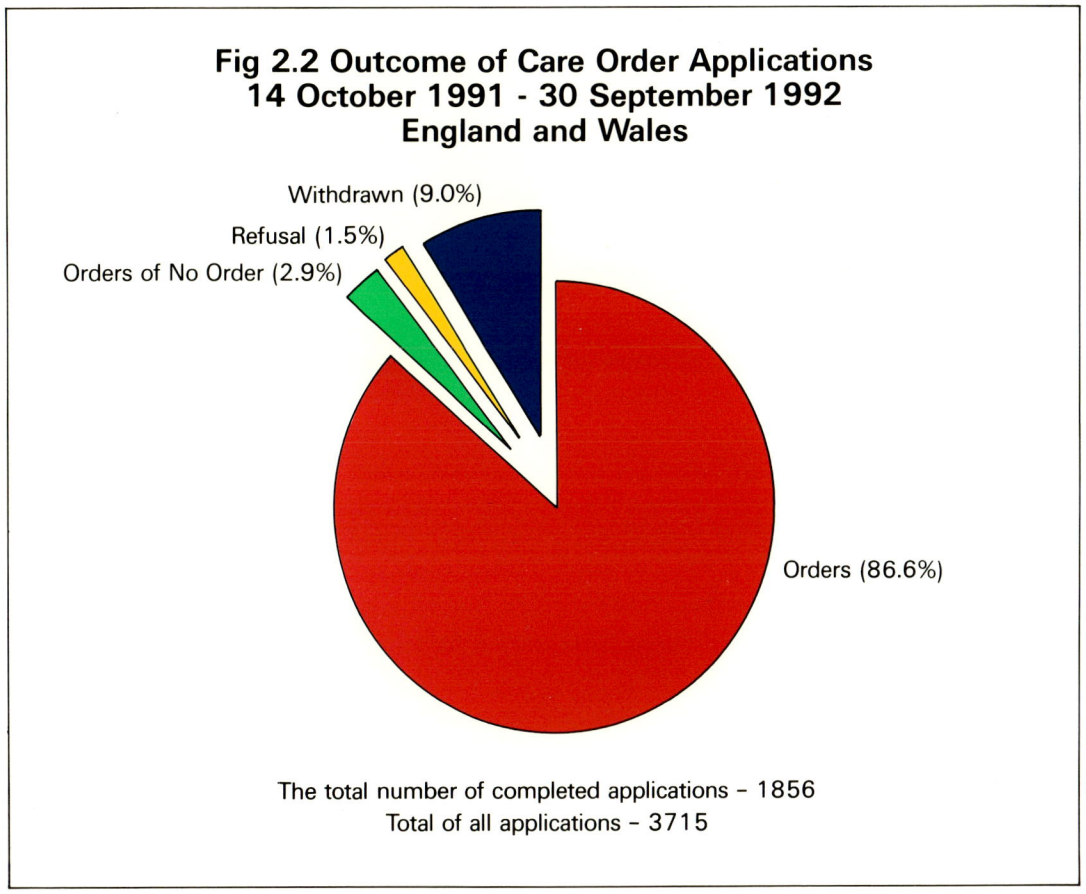

**Fig 2.2 Outcome of Care Order Applications
14 October 1991 - 30 September 1992
England and Wales**

Withdrawn (9.0%)

Refusal (1.5%)

Orders of No Order (2.9%)

Orders (86.6%)

The total number of completed applications – 1856
Total of all applications – 3715

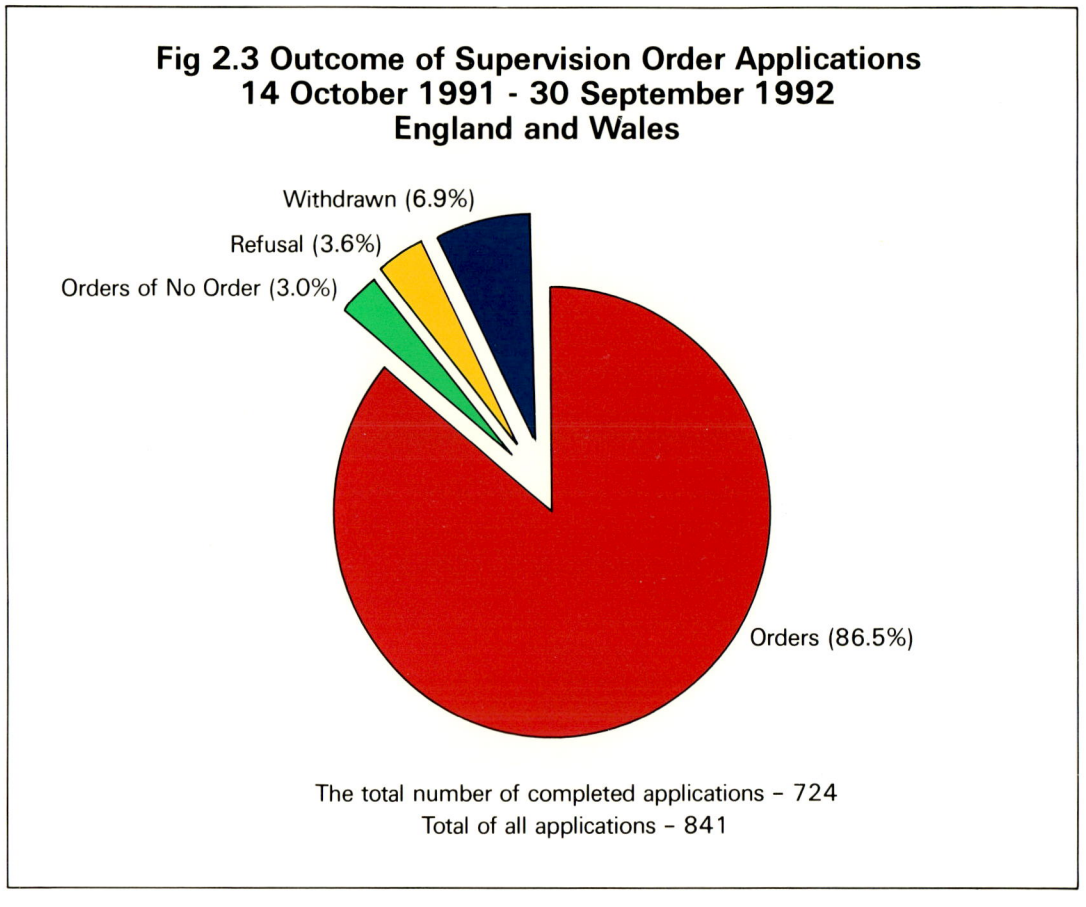

**Fig 2.3 Outcome of Supervision Order Applications
14 October 1991 - 30 September 1992
England and Wales**

Withdrawn (6.9%)

Refusal (3.6%)

Orders of No Order (3.0%)

Orders (86.5%)

The total number of completed applications – 724
Total of all applications – 841

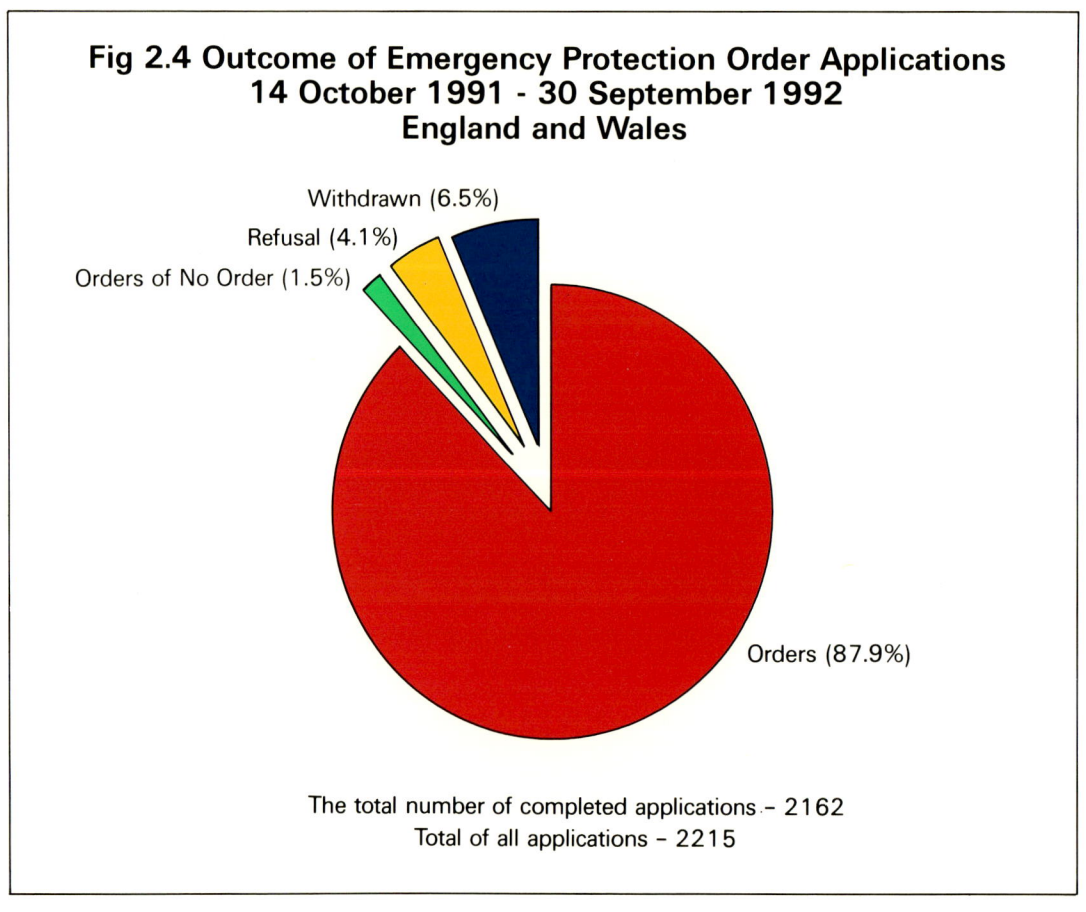

**Fig 2.4 Outcome of Emergency Protection Order Applications
14 October 1991 - 30 September 1992
England and Wales**

Withdrawn (6.5%)

Refusal (4.1%)

Orders of No Order (1.5%)

Orders (87.9%)

The total number of completed applications – 2162
Total of all applications – 2215

Public/Private Law Interface

2.17 The range of orders available to the court in resolving issues around the child's welfare have been widely extended by the Children Act. This has to some extent narrowed the divide between public and private law proceedings. The statistics show that between 14 October 1991 and 30 September 1992 there were 537 directions to investigate a child's circumstances (Section 37) in private law proceedings where the court believed there to have been sufficient concerns to activate the responsible authority's child protection duties. Similarly in public law proceedings use is being made of Section 8 orders as an alternative disposal to a care or supervision order sought by a local authority. There is also anecdotal evidence to suggest that local authorities are themselves encouraging applications for residence and contact orders by members of the extended family in preference to initiating public law proceedings.

2.18 However, the use of Section 8 prohibited steps and specific issues orders by local authorities raises some difficult questions. The Children Act enables local authorities to apply for these only with the leave of the court. Where the need for intervention centres on the alleged abuser of the child, the local authority will always want to explore the possibility of providing services on a voluntary basis, for example, accommodation for the alleged abuser to move away from the family home as an alternative to the removal of the child. Existing legislation makes no public law provision empowering a court to order an alleged abuser out of the home.

Working in Partnership

2.19 While the statistical returns point towards a downturn in court activity as the Act intended, there are genuine concerns to ensure that any shift away from the use of court would not put the child at greater risk. Policy makers, child care professionals and the public at large need to feel confident that the children who appear before the courts do so for the right reasons. Equally, it is important to know that other children whose needs are similar are not excluded from the court process for the 'wrong' reasons.

2.20 A recent SSI study[1] examined these decision making processes in four local authorities in an attempt to address this issue. Arising from the study and Departmental discussions with a number of local authorities was a belief that the 'no order' principle requires authorities to demonstrate that working in partnership has broken down or been exhausted before an order will be made.

2.21 This was not the intention of the legislation. Where a local authority determines that control of the child's circumstances is necessary to promote his welfare then compulsory intervention, as part of a carefully planned process, will always be the appropriate remedy. Local authorities should not feel inhibited by the working in partnership provisions of the Children Act from seeking appropriate court orders. Equally, the existence of a court order should not of itself impede a local authority from continuing its efforts at working in partnership with the families of children in need. The two processes are not mutually exclusive. Each has a role to play, often simultaneously, in the case management of a child at risk.

Emergency Protection Orders

2.22 During the Children Act's passage through Parliament concerns were expressed arising from the Cleveland Inquiry (and others) that too many children were being removed from their homes under place of safety orders and that parental responsibility was being disregarded. The substantially reduced numbers of emergency protection order applications suggest that there has been a shift in practice by local authorities seeking emergency intervention.

2.23 The main features of the new order include:

- limited eight day duration with a possible extension for a further seven days
- right of challenge for certain persons to be heard after 72 hours have elapsed from the making of the order

---

[1] Social Services Inspectorate: Court Orders Study (December 1992)—A Study of Local Authority Decision Making about Public Law Court Applications

- the person obtaining the order has limited parental responsibility
- the court may make directions as to contact with the child or medical/psychiatric examination
- applications may be made in the absence of other interested parties (ie ex-parte).

2.24 These have been limited to what is necessary to protect the child but it remains an extremely serious step. An EPO should not be regarded, as was frequently the case with previous place of safety orders as a routine first step to initiating care proceedings. The new grounds require some evidence that the situation is sufficiently serious to justify the power of intervention being made available.

2.25 However, some local authorities have expressed concerns that courts in some instances have been overly rigid in their interpretation of the procedures for making EPOs.

Points of concern identified in the SSI Court Orders Study are:
- the length of time involved in obtaining the EPO which resulted in the provision being ineffective in the case of an emergency
- once granted the unnecessarily short duration of the order as a means of facilitating the parents right of challenge
- reluctance of the courts to consider ex-parte applications.

2.26 The making of an EPO and its duration should always be governed by what is in the best interests of the child—including allowing the local authority sufficient time to carry out its investigation—so that a child at risk is afforded proper protection through the appropriate court order. Where specific instances of difficulty have come to the attention of the Department of Health these have been followed up through the Lord Chancellor's Department's network of Family Court Business Committees.

2.27 There has been some speculation that reduced court activity might have increased instances where children have been looked after under police protection. Table 2.8 below shows that there were about 400 occasions in the period 14 October 1991 to 31 March 1992 when a child was looked after by a local authority under police protection provisions, or about half the number of instances where a child was looked after under an emergency protection order. Although the incidence of police protection is low, the balance between the two categories is not very different compared to the balance of activity under the previous legislation.

Children Looked After by Local Authorities

2.28 Early estimates from the new Children Looked After return for England suggest that the reduction in court activity has been associated with a marked increase in the numbers of children looked after by local authorities under voluntary agreements. This is in line with what the Act intended.

2.29 Table 2.4 gives details of the estimated number of children looked after by local authorities at 31 March 1992[2]. In total, 55,000 children were looked after: 1,100 children were looked after under care orders or interim orders made under the Act; 32,600 under orders made prior to implementation and now deemed to be made and 2,300 under care orders made under other legislation; 500 children were remanded/detained in local authority accommodation, 100 under emergency protection orders in local authority accommodation. 18,000 were looked after under Section 20 of the Children Act (under voluntary arrangements) and 800 of these were looked after under a series of placements under a single agreement (ie respite care).

2.30 Table 2.5 compares the estimated number of children looked after at 31 March 1992 with the number of children in care at 31 March 1991. These comparisons should be interpreted with care. The legislative change is very considerable and there have also been changes in the data collected. The numbers of children "in care" before the Act was implemented excluded several groups of children that are now "looked after". The biggest groups are children with learning disabilities and other disabled children; others include children under emergency orders, and children bailed to local authority accommodation, and children formerly in local authority care freed for adoption.

---

[2] Estimates for the number of children looked after are based on returns for about 80 authorities which are at various stages of validation. The estimates should be viewed as broad indicators; detailed categories are liable to change.

TABLE 2.4   Estimated numbers of children looked after at 31 March 1992 by legal status

	England
Legal Status	*Number*
All Children looked after	55,000
Interim Orders (S.38 CA 1989)	700
Care Orders (S.31.1a CA 1989)	400
Deemed Care Orders*	32,600
Criminal Care Orders	400
Interim Orders CYPA 1969	600
Interim Wardship	1,300
Emergency Protection Orders	100
Remand/detained in local accommodation	500
S20 (CA 1989) (voluntary arrangements)	18,000
Other	400

*   Orders made under previous legislation and now deemed to be made under the Children Act 1989

CA 1989—Children Act 1989

CYPA 1969—Children and Young Persons Act 1989

Care orders made under CA 1989, include Orders made under S.40 under appeal provisions.

TABLE 2.5   Estimated numbers of children looked after at 31 March 1992 and numbers in care at 31 March 1991 by legal status

	England	
	1992	*1991*
All Children	55,000	59,800
Care Orders	36,000	41,638
S20 (voluntary arrangements)	17,200	
— single placement		17,615
S20 under a series of placements	800	
Remand or detention	500	581
Other	500	*

*   Children under the equivalent of these categories before the Act were not in care.

Children in care at 31 March 1991 have been allocated to the Children Act categories in line with transition provisions of the Act. (For example "care orders" include children under S2 1980 CCA who have been the subject of a rights resolution.)

2.31   Notwithstanding these additional categories the number of children looked after at 31 March 1992 is estimated to be some 5,000 less than the number of children in care at 31 March 1991. Table 2.5 shows the broad categories. At 31 March 1992 36,000 children were looked after under a care order (including care orders deemed to be so under the transitional provisions of the Children Act or interim order). At 31 March 1991, the number of children under a full or interim care order or received into (voluntary) care but subject to a resolution of parental rights (such children become the subject of a deemed order on transition) was 41,500. This category has therefore shown a reduction of some 5,500 over the year confirming that fewer children leave the family home and enter public care.

2.32   The number of children looked after under Section 20 of the Act is slightly greater than the number of children received into care (Section 2 Child Care Act 1980) at 31 March 1991 who had not been the subject of a resolution of parental rights. The additional categories (eg disabled children) can be expected to have had some effect here. This increasing proportion within the total number of children "looked after" by the local authority who are placed under voluntary arrangements is again what the Act intended.

2.33   Tables 2.6 and 2.7 provide preliminary information on the pattern of placement and age breakdown of children looked after by local authorities. The proportion placed in community, voluntary and private homes continues to decline whilst the largest proportional reduction in numbers of children looked after appears to have taken place in the under 5 age group.

Legal status episodes occurring since the Act

2.34   Table 2.8 shows the estimated number of changes to legal status of children looked after occurring between 14 October 1991 and 31 March 1992. This reflects numbers of children starting to be looked after and changes to legal status (renewals of orders alone are not included). Figures for the same period in 1990/91 are also shown for children in care.

2.35   There are two major contrasts between the periods before and after the Act. The number of care order episodes has reduced very considerably—from 5,200 to about 2,000 (including interim and transition episodes) reflecting the changing levels in court activity. But assumptions drawn from this need perhaps to be considered against the time lag effects on the number of care orders made in the period following the Act.

2.36   The number of episodes commencing under Section 20 (voluntary arrangements) is however about double the number of episodes of voluntary care commencing in the same period in 1991. 11,000 episodes commenced under Section 20 under an agreement covering several placements (eg respite care) and 12,200 single placement episodes commenced. The inclusion of episodes reflecting respite care in the 1992 figures does make comparison difficult (especially since one child will often be subject to a number of episodes). Some activity of a similar nature would have been included in the 1991 figures but at a much lower level, because children with disabilities were generally not included in the children in care returns. Nonetheless there does seem to be evidence that the diminishing number of episodes under court orders has been balanced by an increase in "voluntary" provision reflecting increasing cooperation with parents and decreasing recourse to the courts as the Act intended.

TABLE 2.6   Estimated numbers of children looked after by local authorities at 31 March 1992 and number in the care of local authorities at 31 March 1991, by placement

England Numbers and Percentages

	31 March 1992		31 March 1991	
Total	55,000		59,834	
Foster Placements	32,100	58%	34,766	58%
Community Homes				
Registered Voluntary and Private Homes	8,700	16%	10,564	18%
Under placement with parent regulations	6,600	12%	7,297	12%
Other accommodation	7,600	14%	7,207	12%

TABLE 2.7   Estimated numbers of children looked after by a Local Authority at 31 March 1992 and children in care of local authorities at 31 March 1991, by age groups

England

	Under 5	5 and under 10	10 and under 16	16 and 17	Over 17	All Children
Number of children looked after 31.3.92	9,500	12,000	21,300	11,600	600	55,000
Number of children in care 31.3.91	10,807	12,683	23,151	12,798	395	59,834

TABLE 2.8 Legal status episodes commencing between 14 October and 31 March for children in care and children looked after, by legal status

England

Legal Status	1991/92	1990/91
All episodes commencing	27,500	17,973
Interim Care Orders, Care Orders		
including deemed Orders	2,000	5,296
Episodes of Remand or detention	1,000	1,130
Police Protection	400	**
Emergency Protection Orders	700	**
Other	200	**
S.20 CA 1989		11,547
Respite	11,000	
Other	12,200	

** Children under the pre Children Act equivalent of these categories were not in care are not included in Children in care figures.

Includes instances when children start to be looked after or change their legal status.

Working Together

2.37 In October 1991, to coincide with the implementation of the Children Act, the Home Office, the Department of Health, the Department of Education and the Welsh Office revised a guide to arrangements for inter-agency co-operation for the protection of children from abuse. This guide, known as "Working Together"[3] was not intended to be a practice guide for any particular agency or worker. It provided advice on the role of the Area Child Protection Committee; a brief account of some of the legal and ethical considerations which underpin work in child protection; an overview of the roles and organisations and arrangements of the major agencies engaged in child protection work; advice on working together in individual cases; advice on the function and operation of child protection conferences and registers; advice on training in child protection work and advice on reviewing cases.

2.38 Its underlying philosophy and emphasis on inter-agency co-operation was firmly set within the context of the Children Act framework. The main messages of the document were:

- the safety and welfare of the child must be the most important consideration at all times
- an expectation that all work in the area of child protection will be based on inter-agency cooperation
- an expectation that most cases will not require the intervention of the courts and will be dealt with in partnership with the child and family
- an expectation that, except when a child is in acute physical danger, the timing of any removal from home will be considered in the light of the best interests of the child and the need to work in partnership with the whole family
- the need for all those involved in investigative interviews to approach each case with an open mind.

2.39 The Children Act monitoring survey asked a series of questions around the issue of child protection, designed to complement existing management information returns and to establish whether the guidance in "Working Together" was being followed.

Child Protection Registers

2.40 The latest detailed data about child protection registers in England, including category of abuse and age, relate to 31 March 1992. This information had been collected on a regular basis since 1989 following a pilot survey in 1988. In that period the results followed a similar pattern; there was steady upward increase nationally for numbers on the register, registrations and deregistrations. Numbers on the register for example had increased from 41,200 in 1989 to 45,300 in 1991.

---

[3] Working Together under the Children Act 1989—A guide to arrangements for inter-agency co-operation for the protection of children from abuse (HMSO 1991; ISBN 0-11-321472-3).

2.41   When 'Working Together' was published, a significant change was made: the grave concern category (which had been accounting for approximately 50% of registrations) was withdrawn as a category for registration; children already registered were to be reallocated at the next review. Differences in use of the grave concern category was understood to be an important element in the differences in policy and practice between authorities. The possible effect of the withdrawal of this category on the level of registration and numbers on the register was by no means clear. For example, for numbers on the register, the effect would depend on whether children on the register under grave concern were reallocated to another category at the next review or simply removed from the register.

2.42   In the event estimated numbers on the register at 31 March 1992 have shown a reduction of 6,700 (15%) and registrations in the period have fallen by 4,400 (16%); the first reduction in either category since national data has been collected (Table 2.9). Numbers registered under the grave concern category during the year have fallen by 37%, and numbers on the register under the grave concern category have fallen by 38%. These changes have made virtually no difference to the numbers under other categories either for registrations or for numbers on the register. The reduction in the number on the register under 'grave concern' is much less than might have been anticipated and may suggest that some authorities were unable to implement changes to review procedures and systems from 14 October 1991.

2.43   Table 2.10 gives numbers of registrations and numbers of children on the register by age group, for 1991 and 1992. Despite the drop in numbers the pattern by age has remained reasonably constant. There has been a smaller decrease for the age group 10 to 15, both for registrations and for numbers on the register, and for the under one age group on the register. There has been a larger decrease in the age group 16 and over.

2.44   The Department will continue to monitor these figures. It may be that the discipline of having to review the reason for registration, the need to reclassify registrations previously categorised under "Grave Concern" and the emphasis on "partnership" under the Act has had an effect. If so, it is anticipated that the new pattern in numbers on the register and numbers of registrations will continue in future years.

TABLE 2.9   Registration and children on the register by category under which recorded

England

	Registrations including combination categories				On the Registers including combination categories			
	Number and percentages							
	1991		1992		1991		1992	
Total	28,300	100	24,700	100	45,300	100	38,600	100
Neglect	3,300	12	3,700	15	6,800	15	7,300	19
Physical injury	6,700	24	7,100	29	10,600	23	10,900	28
Sexual abuse	3,900	14	4,200	17	6,000	13	6,500	17
Emotional abuse	1,300	5	1,700	7	2,600	6	2,800	7
Grave concern	14,100	50	8,900	36	21,100	47	13,000	34

Numbers on the registers are at 31 March; Registrations are for the year ending 31 March.

Note: The three main categories also feature in the mixed categories. The above table includes these mixed categories with the main categories in order to show the total numbers of children for whom each category of abuse was quoted on the Register. The total of the percentages will exceed 100 because children in the "mixed" categories are counted more than once.

TABLE 2.10   Child Protection Registers: Registration and children on the register by category under which recorded

England

Age[1]	Registrations including combination categories				On the Register including combination categories			
	Numbers and percentages							
	1991		1992		1991		1992	
All ages	28,300	100	24,700	100	45,300	100	38,600	100
Unborn	*	*	200	1	?	?	0[2]	0
Under 1	4,000	14	3,400	14	2,800	6	2,600	7
1–4	8,400	30	7,300	30	14,600	32	12,000	31
5–9	8,000	28	6,600	27	14,500	32	12,200	32
10–15	7,000	25	6,400	26	11,700	26	10,400	27
16 and over	800	3	600	2	1,700	4	1,400	4

Numbers on the registers are at 31 March; Registrations are for the year ending 31 March.
[1] For registrations age at registration, for children on the register age at 31 March 1992.
[2] Less than 50 children.
*   Means not applicable.
    Figures may not add due to rounding.

Unallocated Child Protection Cases

2.45   The placing of children on the child protection register implies:

(i) they are thought to be at risk of a specific form of significant harm

(ii) they are subject to a multi-agency child protection plan

(iii) and that plan is regularly reviewed with the family and revised as change is achieved.

2.46   To secure effective intervention guidance[4] requires that each child on the register must have a named key social worker from either the Social Services Department or the NSPCC. Failure to do so not only prevents progress in carrying out the child protection plan but reduces opportunities for full parental participation and the views of the child to be taken into account in any decision about his or her future.

2.47   As a further response to the Health Select Committee report[5] the monitoring survey asked local authorities for information on unallocated child protection cases. For this purpose a child protection case was categorised as allocated if there was a named social worker who had the responsibility of key worker and undertook the social work aspects of the child protection plan. At 30 June 1992 the total number of unallocated child protection cases in 104 authorities was 1,110 or 3.2% of the total on the Register. Almost 40% of authorities were able to allocate all child protection cases to a social worker. Those that were unable to allocate all cases showed considerable variation. (See figure 2.5).

---

[4] Working Together, Part 5, Paragraph 5.15.2 (page 31).
[5] Second Report from the Health Committee Session 1990–91.

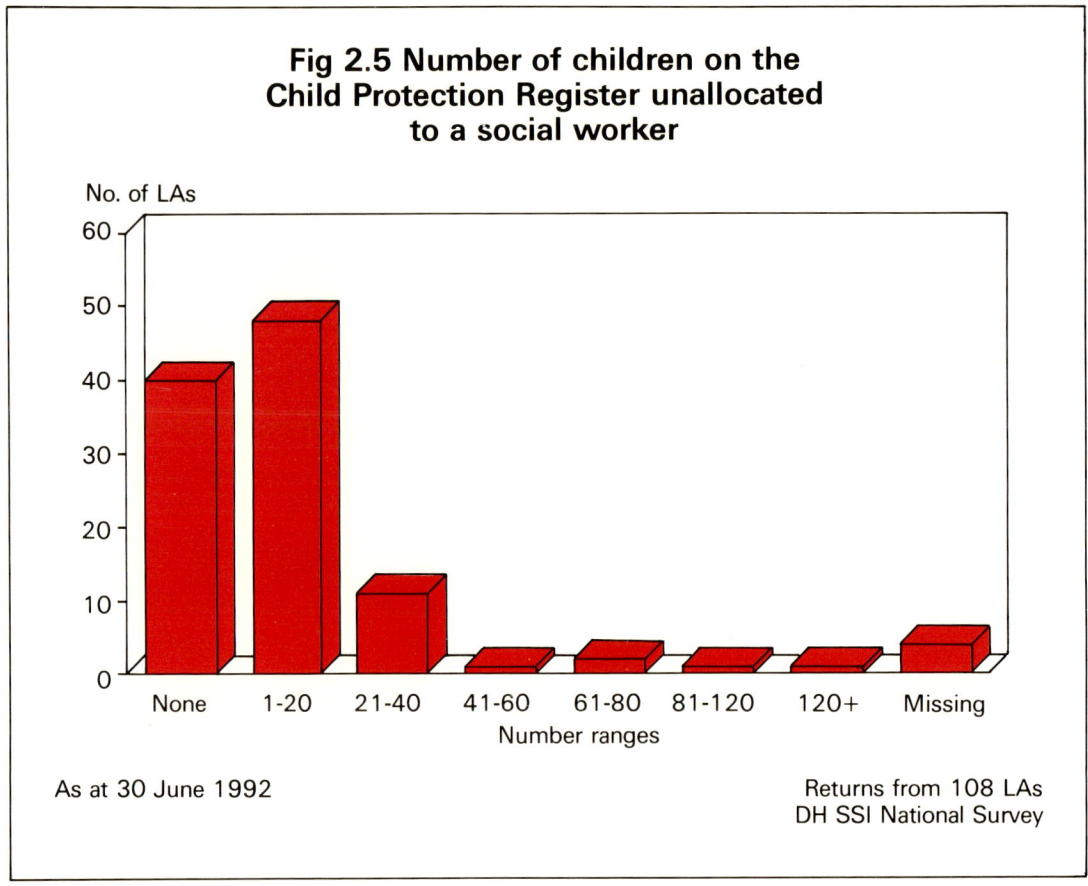

Fig 2.5 Number of children on the Child Protection Register unallocated to a social worker

No. of LAs

As at 30 June 1992

Returns from 108 LAs
DH SSI National Survey

Number ranges

2.48   Twenty six per cent of all unallocated cases were in Inner London authorities. It was possible to compare the returns for this survey with the returns for the survey carried out by the London Region Social Services Inspectorate as at December 1991[6]

2.49   Table 2.11 shows that of the returns received from Inner London authorities there was a reduction of 415 children on Child Protection Registers (11.1%) compared with the previous survey. Only one authority has increased the numbers on the register. There has also been a reduction in the numbers of unallocated cases since the 1991 survey from 381 to 292. There has been a marked improvement in two authorities but a slight increase in the numbers unallocated in four others.

2.50   The Outer London authorities showed a similar overall decrease in the numbers on the Register and in the numbers of children on the Register not allocated to a social worker. This is shown in table 2.12. The majority of the reduction in Outer London authorities is due to Newham having managed to reduce the number of unallocated cases from 114 to 12 at the same time as halving the number of children on the Child Protection Register.

---

[6]   Protecting and Looking After Children: Management Arrangements for Child Care Cases in London published by Department of Health, April 1992.

TABLE 2.11 A comparison of children on the Child Protection Register at 31 December 1991 and 30 June 1992

Inner London

Authority	Children on Child Protection Register 31 December 1991	Children on Child Protection Register 30 June 1992	Children on Child Protection Register not allocated to a social worker 31 December 1991	Children on Child Protection Register not allocated to a social worker 30 June 1992
Camden	N/A	N/A	N/A	N/A
City of London	N/A	0	N/A	0
Hammersmith	112	76	11	1
Kensington	87	77	9	2
Lewisham	318	201	6	8
Southwark	537	443	83	39
Tower Hamlets	216	186	29	11
Greenwich	417	374	69	33
Hackney	160	144	16	30
Islington	237	253	26	26
Lambeth	974	914	132	140
Westminster	N/A	N/A	N/A	N/A
Wandsworth	455	430	0	2
Totals	3,513	3,098	381	292

TABLE 2.12 A comparison of children on the Child Protection Register at 31 December 1991 and 30 June 1992

Outer London

Authority	Children on Child Protection Register 31 December 1991	Children on Child Protection Register 30 June 1992	Children on Child Protection Register not allocated to a social worker 31 December 1991	Children on Child Protection Register not allocated to a social worker 30 June 1992
Barking	136	83	–	2
Barnet	95	106	–	0
Bexley	N/A	0	N/A	0
Brent	245	133	1	4
Bromley	155	107	–	0
Croydon	271	288	11	2
Ealing	N/A	N/A	N/A	N/A
Enfield	141	146	3	0
Haringey	N/A	286	N/A	22
Harrow	131	112	6	8
Havering	118	67	4	12
Hillingdon	149	84	4	1
Hounslow	199	155	9	20
Kingston	48	34	0	0
Merton	150	127	0	0
Newham	388	192	114	12
Redbridge	85	65	0	0
Richmond	82	72	9	2
Sutton	82	86	2	0
Waltham Forest	217	119	0	0
Totals	2,692	2,262	163	85

2.51   Of the total numbers of unallocated cases 34% were in London authorities which have 16% of the total population of children on the Child Protection Register. As has already been noted 39% of authorities were able to allocate all cases to a social worker. Just over two-fifths or 465 of the unallocated cases outside London were in just nine authorities. Table 2.13 shows the numbers of unallocated cases by authority type.

TABLE 2.13   Analysis of the number of authorities with unallocated child Protection Register cases at 30 June 1992

	Inner London	Outer London	Metro-politan Authorities	Shire counties	Total
Number of authorities with no unallocated child protection cases	1	9	14	16	40
Number of authorities with less than 5 unallocated child protection cases	3	5	4	9	21
Number of authorities with 5 but less than 20 unallocated child protection cases	2	3	11	10	26
Number of authorities with 20 or more unallocated child protection cases	5	2	6	4	17
No return	2	1	1	0	4
Total	13	20	36	39	108

2.52   It was reported that 263 (23.7%) of the child protection cases which were not allocated to a social worker had been unallocated for over three months. Of these 239 (91%) were in the 17 local authorities with the highest numbers of unallocated cases. The fact that the largest proportion of unallocated cases over three months were in a very few authorities suggests that in those authorities there may be an underlying structural problem which needs to be tackled by management action.

Management responsibility for unallocated cases

2.53   Questions were asked in the monitoring survey which were designed to find out at what level of management information on unallocated cases was held and who had responsibility for taking action to ensure that the unallocated were allocated as soon as possible. There was no clear link between the level of management that received information and whether or not an authority had unallocated cases. Some authorities with higher numbers of unallocated Child Protection cases did not appear to have any system in place for information gathering, monitoring of the position or a clearly designated line of responsibility for action at officer level. In most authorities the information was received by both middle and senior management and one or other level had responsibility for taking action. In five of the 17 authorities with the highest numbers of unallocated cases the information was reported to the Social Services Committee. In 3 of the 17 the Social Services Committee took responsibility for action. In over half of the responses the information was passed to the Area Child Protection Committee although only 9 Area Child Protection Committees were reported to have any responsibility for taking action. In most cases (61%) the responsibility for action rested at Senior Manager level.

2.54   Area Child Protection Committees are a recognised joint forum for developing, monitoring and reviewing child protection policies. Cooperation at the individual case level needs to be supported by joint agency and management policies for child protection. There was no apparent correlation between high or low numbers on the register and likelihood that the Area Child Protection Committee would receive information about unallocated cases. Of the 10 Area Child Protection Committees which had responsibility for action on unallocated cases 7 had such cases and 3 had none.

Procedures

2.55   Under the circular which was sent out at the same time as Working Together (LAC(91)17) Area Child Protection Committees were required to revise their procedures in the light of the Children Act and Working Together and to have the new procedures in place within a year of the circular. Almost 43% of authorities reported that they had at 30 June 1992 revised their procedure in the light of Working Together and all expected to issue revised procedures by April 1993. The survey did not collect information on the quality of the revised procedures nor on whether or not they matched the requirements set out in Appendix 6 of Working Together.

Wales

2.56   The numbers of children on registers in Wales have declined from 2,460 to 2,112 between 31 March 1991 and 31 March 1992. At most times, local authorities are able to ensure that all such children have a social worker allocated to them. There are currently no unallocated cases.

Unallocated Children "Looked After" Cases

2.57   Although the Select Health Committee Report recommended that the Social Services Inspectorate review of unallocated child protection cases only should be extended nationwide, the national monitoring survey asked local authorities for additional information on unallocated children looked after cases.

2.58   The new Regulations and Guidance issued in the Children Act series (in particular Volume 3) lists a range of duties and requirements for local authorities in respect of children looked after by them. Inquiries have to be undertaken prior to placement and arrangements agreed with those holding parental responsibility; children in placements (especially in foster care) must be visited at prescribed minimum intervals; the continued suitability of the placements and placement objectives must be reviewed at prescribed intervals. These essential tasks cannot be achieved without having a social worker allocated to the case. The essential principles enacted by Parliament—parental participation; due regard to issues of race and culture; seeking out the wishes and feelings of the child—are all in jeopardy unless the case is allocated.

2.59   As at 30 June 1992 the total number of unallocated children looked after cases was 1,543 or 2.9% of the total numbers of children looked after. In 31 authorities all children looked after cases were allocated to a social worker. Those authorities that were unable to allocate all cases showed even more variation than for unallocated child protection cases (see figure 2.6). It is of particular concern that just three authorities between them accounted for two fifths of all unallocated children looked after cases—with numbers ranging from 164 to 239 per authority. Table 2.14 shows the distribution of such cases by type of authority. The London authorities account for two fifths of unallocated looked after cases but only 16.7% of the number of children looked after.

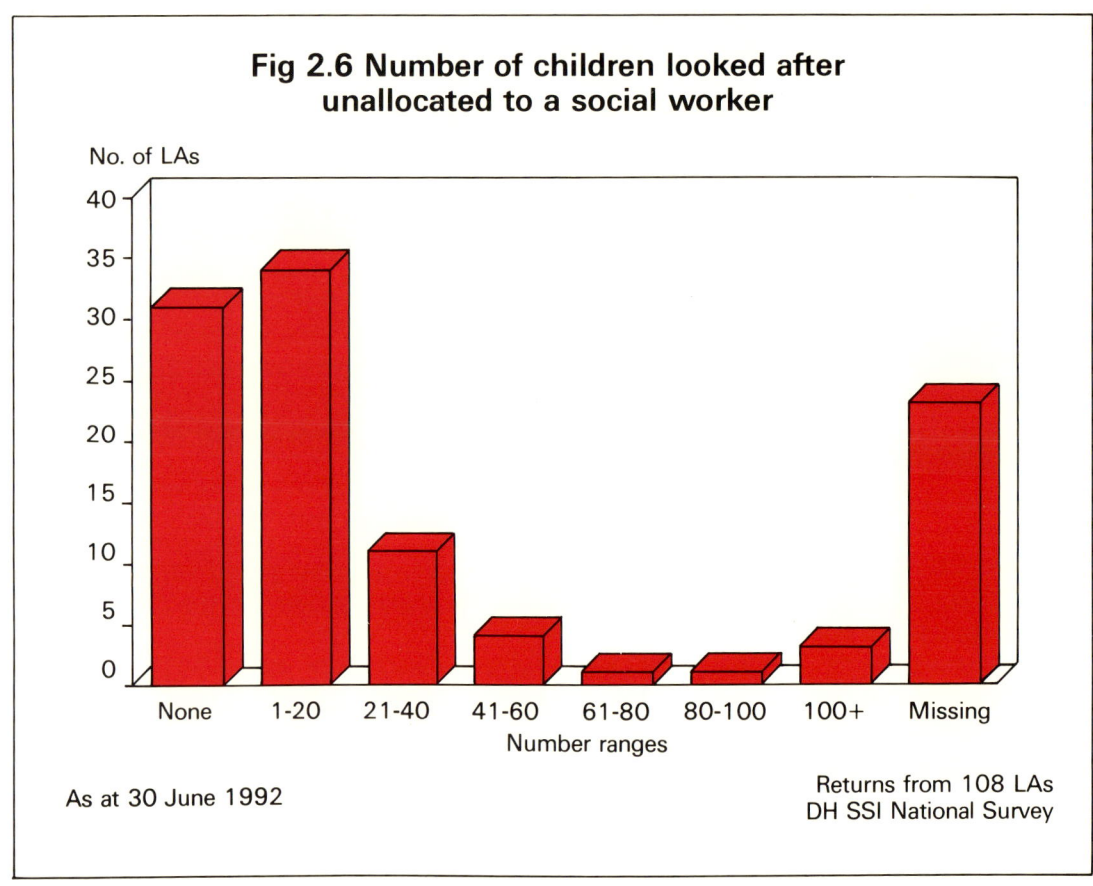

Fig 2.6 Number of children looked after unallocated to a social worker

No. of LAs

As at 30 June 1992

Returns from 108 LAs
DH SSI National Survey

TABLE 2.14   Number of Authorities with unallocated children looked after cases at 30 June 1992

	Inner London	Outer London	Metro-politan Authorities	Shire counties	Total
Number of authorities with no unallocated children looked after	3	6	7	15	31
Number of authorities with less than 5 unallocated children looked after	0	4	3	5	12
Number of authorities with 5 but less than 30 unallocated children looked after	4	5	11	8	28
Number of authorities with 30 or more unallocated children looked after	3	3	4	4	14
No return	3	2	11	7	13
Total	13	20	36	39	108

2.60   Tables 2.15 and 2.16 chart the movements in numbers of children looked after and those not allocated to a social worker in London authorities between 31 December 1991 and 30 June 1992. For the majority of authorities, where comparable data is available, there has been an encouraging fall in the numbers of unallocated children looked after cases. Most notable is Greenwich where the proportion of such cases has dropped from a third of all children looked after in the authority to just 5%. It is of considerable concern, however, to note the dramatic increase in Southwark where the number of unallocated cases has risen to 164, that is, a quarter of the authority's looked after children and just over a quarter of all unallocated children looked after cases in London.

TABLE 2.15 A comparison of numbers of children looked after between 31 December 1991 and 30 June 1992

Inner London

	Number of children looked after at 31 December 1991	Number of children looked after at 30 June 1992	Number of children looked after not allocated to a social worker at 31 December 1991	Number of children looked after not allocated to a social worker at 30 June 1992
Camden	N/A	316	N/A	N/A
City of London	1	1	0	0
Hammersmith	308	244	4	6
Kensington	191	210	3	0
Lewisham	536	540	20	0
Southwark	576	667	66	164
Tower Hamlets	314	306	5	N/A
Greenwich	458	369	150	20
Hackney	615	533	70	15
Islington	414	414	39	39
Lambeth	721	726	106	95
Westminster	277	N/A	5	N/A
Wandsworth	447	433	39	25
Total	4,858	4,759	507	364

TABLE 2.16 A comparison of numbers of children looked after between 31 December 1991 and 30 June 1992

Outer London

	Number of children looked after at 31 December 1991	Number of children looked after at 30 June 1992	Number of children looked after not allocated to a social worker at 31 December 1991	Number of children looked after not allocated to a social worker at 30 June 1992
Barking	197	199	6	1
Barnet	153	191	0	0
Bexley	157	158	0	0
Brent	438	408	2	N/A
Bromley	205	221	0	0
Croydon	344	362	22	15
Ealing	396	N/A	12	N/A
Enfield	175	222	8	13
Haringey	423	511	64	49
Harrow	127	145	3	2
Havering	150	144	0	22
Hillingdon	155	155	0	0
Hounslow	266	273	77	42
Kingston	154	132	6	6
Merton	145	218	1	1
Newham	501	312	N/A	70
Redbridge	118	122	0	0
Richmond	88	80	6	4
Sutton	130	127	0	0
Waltham Forest	331	265	0	11
Total	4,653	4,245	207	236

2.61   463 cases or 30% of the 1,543 unallocated looked after cases had been unallocated for more than three months. There was no obvious relationship between the numbers unallocated and the length of time the cases have been unallocated. On the other hand the survey suggests that if an authority has high numbers of unallocated child protection cases they are more likely to have high numbers of unallocated cases of children being looked after or accommodated by the local authority. Almost half of the children being looked after by the local authority who were not allocated to a social worker were in those authorities which had also recorded the highest numbers of unallocated child protection cases. There was, however, one significant exception. The authority with the highest recorded number of unallocated children looked after cases had only 16 child protection cases unallocated to a social worker, two of which had been unallocated over three months. This may suggest that in that authority high priority is being given to child protection work. It should be said, however, most children on the Child Protection Register are not children being looked after and it is likely that those who are being looked after would be the more difficult, complex cases who might expect to have been allocated to a social worker as a matter of priority.

General

2.62   The Department recognises that at any point in time there may be a few cases that have not yet been allocated to a social worker but this should never be allowed to drift for more than a short period. The Social Services Inspectorate will continue to monitor closely the authorities which appear to have a chronic problem, that is large numbers of unallocated cases and those with cases unallocated to a social worker for more than three months. Arising from the most recent London Region SSI survey London authorities identified as giving cause for concern were asked to furnish a report to SSI, on the steps needed or being taken to bring improvement to the child protection and children looked after services. Reports were received during September 1992 and based on an assessment of progress further full reports were requested from Lambeth, Camden, Southwark, Greenwich and Haringey after a further six months. A similar programme of work will be undertaken with authorities presenting serious problems in the rest of the country as revealed by the Children Act national monitoring survey. A detailed analysis of the national survey returns for both unallocated child protection and children looked after cases will be published by the SSI later in the year.

Chapter 3: Family Support Services for Children in Need

Background

3.1   The Children Act is based on a clear set of principles, drawing in particular on parental responsibility and non-intervention in family life unless necessary. When support within a family fails or is absent, the local authority has a duty to offer aid to the family or directly to the child to promote his welfare. The responsible authority must then withdraw when parents are again able to discharge fully their responsibilities to their children. Such support services need to be seen as acceptable, non-stigmatised responses to the normal problems of family life.

3.2   Part III of the Act provides the legal framework by which these principles are made explicit. Local authorities have a general duty to provide a range and level of services appropriate to the needs of the children in their area so as to safeguard and promote their welfare and, so far as is consistent with that aim, promote their upbringing by their families.

3.3   The definition of children "in need" in the Children Act has been cast deliberately wide. It has three "limbs" referring to (i) children who are unlikely to achieve or maintain a reasonable standard of health and development without the provision of services; (ii) children whose health or development is likely to be significantly impaired, or further impaired, without the provision of services; and (iii) disabled children. Although not expected to meet every need, local authorities are required to identify the extent of local need and then make decisions on priorities for service provision in the context of that information, their statutory duties and resources.

3.4   Research on children-in-need[1] undertaken on behalf of the Department of Health suggests that the implementation process in this key area is gradually being carried forward by many local authorities. However, some are being rather slow to develop adequate children-in-need initiatives and are finding it difficult to move from a social policing to a more proactive partnership role. The findings of the research project, which form the basis of this section of the report, rely on a 55% response rate from 60 local authorities in England only, considerably fewer than responded to the national monitoring survey covering other areas of the Act. It is possible that these 60 local authorities are over representative of those carrying forward the new legislative requirements, in which case the findings will overestimate the extent of compliance with Part III of the Act. The Welsh Office has grant aided, through West Glamorgan County Council, a research project to be undertaken over 3 years by Dr Matthew Colton of Swansea University to evaluate the provision of services by local authorities in Wales to children in need.

Defining Children in Need

3.5   Authorities were asked by the researchers about their implementation of services on two levels. Firstly whether they had used data in determining the extent of need to establish priority groups for service delivery, and also how they might prioritise services in relation to individual children referred to them.

3.6   The predominant method used by authorities to establish the *numbers* of children in need was a mixture of referrals and membership of a pre-determined group (for example children with unemployed parents, homeless families, disabled children, drug abusing children, young people in trouble with or at risk of being in trouble with the law). Information on the extent of need has largely been collected through in-house research, but many social services departments are also engaging in a wide ranging consultation process with local and national agencies and other departments within the local authority. Some authorities are also using government statistics and reports from agencies, for example, the Audit Commission. Others anticipate using data from the 1991 census when available.

---

[1]   National Monitoring of the Children Act: Part III section 17—the first year. Dr Jane Aldgate/Ms Jane Tunstill/Graham McBeath—Oxford University/NCVCCO.

3.7 Nearly all the authorities who replied had adopted a common system for prioritising levels of need entitling access to services. In some, these had been agreed with other departments and agencies especially education, housing, leisure and district health authorities. Some had also reached agreements with family health services, probation and voluntary agencies.

3.8 It was clear that the highest priority was accorded to children for whom authorities already had some existing responsibility eg children at risk of significant harm, at risk of neglect, in accommodation or care. When describing their approach to children in the community as opposed to those for whom they already had some responsibility, there was less general acceptance that such children constituted pre-determined groups (except for children with disabilities).

3.9 As table 3.1 shows, in relation to the first "limb" of the children in need definition only 23 local authorities identified children with special health needs as "in need". This poor showing may reflect the need for health services to be more proactive through their screening and surveillance programmes in bringing children with special health needs to the attention of social services. Similarly 19 authorities grouped drug/solvent abusing children. While only 21 authorities recognised children at risk of HIV/AIDS, it could be argued that this was a new group which needed planning for, and as such the figure of 21 could be regarded as encouraging, as compared with school truants which are an established yet low rated group. Only 9 authorities regarded truants and 15 authorities regarded children excluded from school as children in need. It was noticeable that just over a third considered children with difficult family relations, and 19 and 10 respectively considered children of homeless, and unemployed parents, to be a pre-determined group of children in need. 17 saw children in families living in bed and breakfast accommodation, and 8 saw children in families whose gas, electricity or water had been disconnected, as predetermined groups of children in need.

TABLE 3.1 Ranked scores for pre-determined groups of "children in the community" used in identifying the extent of children in need under the first limb of the "in-need" definition.

Rank	Group	No of LA's using group identifier
1.	Children with special education needs.	27
2.	Children with special health needs.	23
2.	Children with difficult family relationships.	23
3.	Young people in the penal system.	22
4.	Children at risk of/who have HIV/AIDS.	21
4.	Children with Disabilities.	21
5.	Homeless families.	19
5.	Drug/Solvent abusing children.	19
6.	Carers with disabilities.	18
7.	Families in Bed and Breakfast Accomm.	17
8.	Children excluded from school.	15
8.	Children living in substandard housing.	15
8.	Children in low income families.	15
8.	Carers with mental illness.	15
9.	Young people in Bed and Breakfast Accomm.	14
10.	Children in specific geographical areas.	12
10.	One parent families	12
11.	Refugee families	12
12.	Black/ethnic minority families.	10
12.	Children under 8.	10
12.	Unemployed parents.	10
13.	School Truants.	9
14.	Families whose gas/electricity/water has been disconnected.	8
15.	Children of divorcing parents.	7
16.	Adopted Children	6
16.	Children with English as second language.	5
18.	Children in Independent Schools.	4

Source: Aldgate/Tunstill/McBeath research   No of returns = 60

3.10   It is of some concern that such low priority is given to these groups in signalling either access, to or developing, services. The Children Act represents a move away from the provision of support services as a reactive measure to prevent a child coming into care towards a proactive programme of support for children in need and their families. The task for local authorities is to develop coherent strategies of support in order to respond appropriately to local needs.

Consultation Process

3.11   A local authority may request certain other persons to help in the exercise of their functions under Part III of the Act. These include any other local authority, a health authority, a local housing authority or a local education authority. Guidance[2] recommends that local authorities develop a corporate policy and clear departmental procedures in respect of inter-departmental collaboration to ensure good cooperation at all levels. This implies a need for good and extensive planning and consultation.

3.12   Only half of the social services departments indicated that they had held meetings with staff within various sections of the department. This may mean that there is insufficient in-service training or policy dissemination to practitioners involved with implementation of the Act.

3.13   Consultation between departments within local authorities was significantly better. There was a wide distribution of discussion documents to education, leisure, recreation and housing departments. Most local authorities found contributions positive although some felt that housing and leisure could have been more helpful. Consultation with health services, police and probation was generally regarded as productive.

3.14   It is disappointing to note that only half the authorities who responded had consultations with voluntary organisations but nearly all those who did felt that these had been valuable. There was a low level of consultation with interested local community and parents groups; in the main it was contacts with local branches of national voluntary agencies which were used. While these contacts are important, the kind of data bases and expertise available at a local level may not offer such a comprehensive view of policy and services as that held at national headquarters or that held by specifically local agencies.

Service Provision

3.15   The returns indicate nevertheless that most authorities are providing a range of services commensurate with the purposes of the Children Act. Some authorities have found that they are being delayed by factors outside their control such as the development of new information systems and computer services, but on the whole these teething problems are being surmounted and important data such as demographic materials, locally emerging factors of need and the extent of children in need is being gathered. Where there were reported shortfalls in service provision, it is clear that efforts are being made to introduce new services, as shown in Table 3.2.

---

[2]   The Children Act 1989: Guidance & Regulations Volume 2 Family Support, Day Care & Educational Provision for Young Children paragraph 1.13.

TABLE 3.2   Present and Future Services

Service	Able to Offer	Introduce/ Develop
Day nurseries	48	6
Family centres	50	27
Home visiting	49	9
Befriending	30	11
Family aides	45	19
Domiciliary care	56	17
Laundry services	29	6
Sponsored child minding	53	16
Child protection	58	11
Advice/counselling to parents	55	12
Advice/counselling to children	56	20
Preparing children with disabilities for independence	47	31
Child guidance/psychiatry	49	8
Supervision for matrimonial cases	37	3
Respite care general	52	24
Respite care for disabled	59	27
Full time accommodation (general)	59	10
Full time accommodation (disabled)	54	14
Foster care	58	17
Accommodation for those ceasing to be looked after	52	24
Education for those looked after	32	19
After school care	31	29
Holiday activities	41	22
Supervised activities	54	12
Transport	53	8
Help to enable a holiday	39	5
Financial payments under section 17	58	13

Source: Aldgate/Tunstill/McBeath research   No of returns = 60

3.16   There is a particularly strong showing on the provision of family centres, day nurseries, child protection services, respite care, short and longer term accommodation for children with disabilities, accommodation for children ceasing to be looked after and financial payments under S17 to meet exceptional needs. Again, on the evidence obtained to date, at least half of the authorities are providing additional educational services for children looked after and out of school care, and most are providing a range of supervised activities.

3.17   In May 1992 SSI published the results of a survey they had undertaken of the provision of family centres in Wales by both local authorities and the voluntary sector. 28 family centres and 9 child and family psychiatric centres were identified. The SSI report gave details of the centres' management arrangements, funding sources and service delivery activities.

3.18   The Act requires that authorities should facilitate the provision by others, including voluntary organisations, of services which they have the powers to provide under Part III of the Act. This implies that services will be provided for children in need by a multiplicity of agencies and will not solely be the responsibility of social services departments. Indications of the extent of diversification in service delivery are illustrated in table 3.3.

TABLE 3.3   Service Provision – some examples

Service	SSD	Other LA Dept.	Voluntary Agency	Private Company	Ad Hoc
Day nursery	41	14	10	5	27
Family centres	42	2	30	0	7
Guidance for disabled children and their parents	57	20	25	0	5
Guidance to parents general	58	14	25	0	4
Preparing disabled children for independence	54	25	11	0	7
Respite care general	55	3	8	0	19
Respite care for disabled children	58	5	23	3	22
Full time accommodation general	58	4	15	6	37
Full time accommodation for disabled children	48	10	16	5	33
Foster care	58	1	7	0	16
After school care	17	26	11	4	15
Holiday activities	26	35	20	3	20

Source: Aldgate/Tunstill research   No of returns = 60

3.19   Use of voluntary organisations proved the most popular alternative to direct provision by social services departments. In many cases services are being provided by a department other than the social services department within a local authority. Few local authorities are using private companies for any services and authorities quite often engage in ad hoc arrangements with outside agencies to provide certain types of services such as day nurseries and the various forms of accommodation of children looked after by the authority.

3.20   This decentralisation of service delivery is an encouraging sign that partnerships with outside bodies are continuing to develop. This in turn should lead to further social services initiatives based on a greater degree of shared information, planning and resourcing and a diminished reliance on ad hoc arrangements.

Children with Disabilities

3.21   By including children with disabilities in the definition of "in need", the Children Act integrates legislation about local authorities' responsibilities for disabled children with other children who are or may be in need. Under previous legislation for example a disabled child living away from home only received the same level of protection from the local authority as other children if he was taken into care. The Act now requires authorities to provide for aspects of a disabled child's development, as well as providing practical services where necessary to overcome the effects of his or her disability. The Act treats a child with a disability as a child first, albeit a child who may additionally have very special needs.

3.22   The Act places a duty on local authorities to keep a separate register of children with disabilities in their area, to assist in service planning and monitoring. They must also provide services to minimise the effect of their disabilities and to give such children the opportunity to lead lives which are as normal as possible. Guidance[3] stresses the importance of agencies working together in the provision of services for children with disabilities. This encouragement to collaboration between authorities is designed to ensure that authorities see children "in the round" and do not look at specific needs in isolation. It should also ensure that parents and children are not subject to a confusing variety of assessment procedures.

---

[3]   The Children Act 1989 Guidance and Regulations Volume 6: Children with Disabilities. Chapter 4: Co-ordinating services.

Register of children with disabilities

3.23 The national monitoring survey revealed that by June 1992 one third of local authorities had yet to complete their arrangements for maintaining a register of children with disabilities. This is disappointing and is a matter for concern since, under previous legislation, local authorities had to register adults with disabilities (and it was open to them to register children if they wished).

3.24 In those areas where arrangements are in place, the register is maintained in a majority of cases by social services. In other areas the social services department shares the task with health and/or education authorities; none share the task with a voluntary organisation. Two authorities reported that the register was maintained jointly between the local health authority and other agency

TABLE 3.4 Who keeps the Register of Children with Disabilities?

	Number	%
SSD	45	41.7
Health Authority	11	10.2
Education Authority	1	0.9
Other	3	2.8
SSD & Health Authority	6	5.6
SSD & Education Authority	2	1.9
SSD and voluntary organisation	0	0
SSD, Health & Education Authorities	5	4.6
Not yet set up	35	32.4

Source: DH SSI national survey June 1992   No of returns = 108

3.25 In establishing registers of disabled children, guidance[4] emphasises that criteria for definitions of disability are best decided in discussion between health, education and social services, on the basis that the creation of a joint register would greatly facilitate collaboration in identification and a co-ordinated provision of service.

3.26 The involvement of voluntary agencies in the process of establishing disability criteria is not mandatory, their role being one of participation in service planning. However, the voluntary agencies have much to offer in terms of knowledge and expertise and could be used productively in this area.

3.27 Two thirds of social services departments indicated they had agreed common criteria with other departments in the local authority for registration of children with disabilities. About two fifths of authorities had worked out criteria with local or national voluntary organisations. Table 3.5 illustrates this.

TABLE 3.5 Agreement of Common Criteria with other Departments for inclusion on the Register of Disabled Children

Health	43
Education	41
Voluntary Sector	24
Other	9

Source: Aldgate/Tunstill/McBeath research

Most commonly reported was agreement reached with health authorities—although surprisingly perhaps, this was not the case in all responding authorities—education authorities and the voluntary sector.

Service provision

3.28 Authorities were asked by researchers what services they were able to offer specifically for children with disabilities, which of these they wished to develop further, and which they would like to introduce. These are described in table 3.6.

---

[4]   The Children Act 1989 Guidance and Regulations Volume 6: Children with Disabilities. Chapter 4: Co-Ordinating Services.

TABLE 3.6   Present and Future Services

Service	Able to Offer	Introduce/ Develop
Advice/counselling to children with disabilities and their parents	56	20
Preparing children with disabilities for independence	47	31
Respite care for children with disabilities	59	27
Full time accommodation for children with disabilities	54	14

Source: Aldgate/Tunstill/McBeath research   No of returns = 60

Short-term accommodation for children with disabilities

3.29   Guidance[5] recommends that short term accommodation be provided in the context of a planned package of care, for children with disabilities and 53 of the authorities who replied offered this type of service provision and did so for all age groups. However, 24 authorities offered it as relief care only, with no other services, while a further 8 provide a "crash pad" emergency service.

3.30   Since implementation representations have been made to the Department of Health about the impact of the new Regulations on episodes of short term foster care for children with disabilities. In the past, these arrangements tended to be relatively informal and spontaneous. Concern has been expressed that the service for these children may now be over-formalised and over-regulated. On the other hand others have expressed satisfaction that the new arrangements do far more to ensure that placements are safe and satisfactory and conducted with full parental participation. Respite carers (foster parents) have reported that they feel their work is more fully recognised. The Department of Health in collaboration with Barnardos mounted a national seminar on the issue of respite care in January 1993.

3.31   Table 3.7 suggests that the decentralisation of service delivery to children with disabilities is similar to that for services to children in need generally.

TABLE 3.7   Service Providers for Children with Disabilities

Service	SSD	Other LA Dept.	Voluntary Agency	Private Company	Ad Hoc
Guidance for children with disabilities and their parents	57	20	25	0	5
Preparing disabled children for independence	54	25	11	0	7
Respite care for children with disabilities	58	5	23	3	22
Full time accommodation for children with disabilities	48	10	16	5	33

Source: Aldgate/Tunstill/McBeath research   No of returns = 60

---

[5]   The Children Act 1989 Guidance and Regulations Volume 6: Children with Disabilities. Chapter 6: Assessment and planning process.

Liaison between SSDs, education departments and health authorities over service provision

3.32   The extent of implementation of Part III and Schedule 2 of the Act, as regards inter-agency co-operation for all children in need is shown in Table 3.8.

TABLE 3.8   Inter-Agency co-operation

	Children with disabilities	*Other children*
(a) Named senior officer in social services and education departments and health authorities responsible for liaison on services for children	86	59
(b) Regular meetings of senior managers with responsibility for children	79	53
(c) SSD officer responsible for receipt of notification of children accommodated[6]	73	12
a+b	73	47
b+c	58	7
a+c	64	7

Source: DH SSI national survey June 1992   No of returns = 96

Children with Disabilities in Wales

3.33   The Social Services Inspectorate Wales published a survey of the organisation of social services for children with disabilities in October 1992. Most services for children with disabilities are being provided through teams focusing on disability. Access to general children's services is patchy. Social services departments have begun to address issues about how to ensure that children with disabilities are dealt with as children first whilst making sure that their special needs are met. The Inspectorate has development work planned for early 1993 to assist authorities in taking their work forward.

3.34   At the time the survey was undertaken some inter-agency arrangements were in place for planning services for children with a disability as part of planning services for adults with a disability; some inter-agency arrangements were in place for individual planning.

3.35   Inter-agency co-operation is evident in work being undertaken to develop registers of children with disabilities. In seven counties in Wales the social services department, education department and health authority have been working together to develop a system which will provide as comprehensive a register of children with disabilities as possible. Of these, one county has a manual register in operation; it is piloting a computer system. In another county there is an interim arrangement with the health authority to use its register of children with disabilities, pending completion of outer-agency plans for a register.

3.36   A third county in Wales is collating information held by the social services and education departments and the health authority and should have a register in operation early in 1993. The other four counties are at various stages in developing a system for the register. One has the framework complete but has to complete plans for implementation. In the eighth county the social services department is developing the register as part of its departmental information system; it is in consultation with the education department and health authority. In the meantime, both the social services and education departments hold information about children with disabilities.

---

[6]   Sections 85 and 86 of the Act refer to children accommodated for more than 3 months by health authorities, LEAs, residential care homes, nursing or mental nursing homes.

Access to Services and Publicity

3.37   To enable parents and children to participate fully with authorities in making decisions about the services they wish to have and the processes by which they are delivered, families need to be aware of the range of services on offer and the routes by which they can be accessed. Local authorities are required to publish information about the services they provide themselves and where appropriate those provided by others. Publicity material should be sensitive to the needs of potential users, and in particular take account of ethnic minorities' cultural and linguistic needs and the needs of those with sensory disabilities.

3.38   The findings from the national survey revealed that a good deal of effort had been put into this by social services. Popular and effective locations for displaying their publicised services included public libraries, GP surgeries, Citizens Advice Bureaux and Family Centres. Some authorities have circularised local solicitors and places of worship, others have provided articles for borough magazines. Table 3.9 illustrates the steps taken by local authorities to inform and advise potential users of a sample of services.

TABLE 3.9   Steps taken by Local Authorities to inform and advise potential users of a sample of services

Service	Leaflet/ Guide-book produced or in preparation	Helpline or Helpdesk	Media coverage	Infor- mation network set up	Other
General services for children in need	90	16	30	14	16
Day care	91	15	25	29	9
Services for children and young people with disabilities	77	13	10	19	14
Services offered by local voluntary or independent organisations	51	10	8	19	14
Provision of accommodation	73	6	5	9	6
Advice and assistance for those ceasing to be looked after	77	9	9	17	13
Transport	15	5	0	4	2
Child Protection	83	19	24	16	7

Source: DH SSI national survey   No of returns = 108

3.39   Of the services listed in Table 3.9:

(i) general services for children in need;

(ii) day care;

(iii) services for children/young persons with disabilities;

(iv) services offered by local voluntary or independent organisations

particularly represent new changes brought in under the Children Act. It is encouraging to note that 36 authorities publicise these particular services by more than four different means.

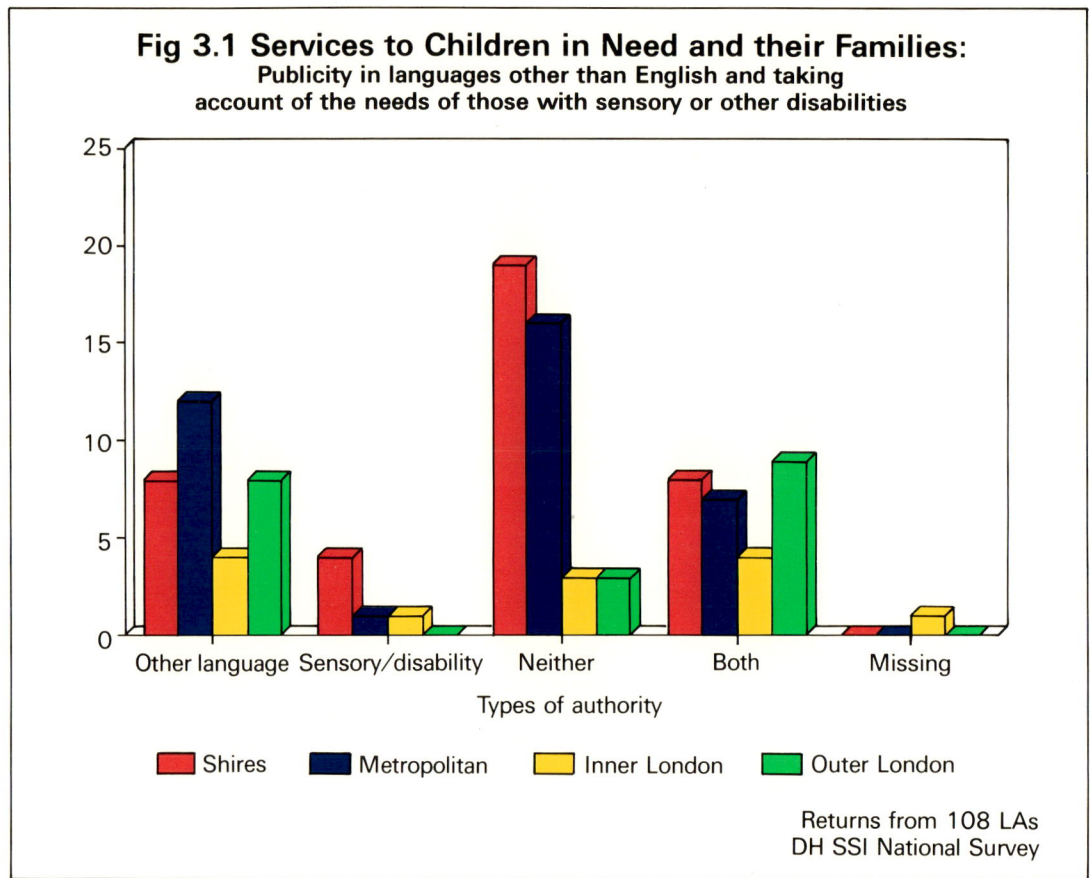

Fig 3.1 Services to Children in Need and their Families:
Publicity in languages other than English and taking
account of the needs of those with sensory or other disabilities

Types of authority

■ Shires ■ Metropolitan ☐ Inner London ■ Outer London

Returns from 108 LAs
DH SSI National Survey

3.40   Figure 3.1 shows the extent to which different types of authority publicise their services in languages other than English and/or taking account of the needs of those with sensory or other disabilities. Altogether 60 local authorities publicised their services in at least one other language and 34 did so in ways which take account of particular disabilities.

3.41   In Wales printed material (newsletters, leaflets, booklets) are most commonly used to give information about services. In 2 counties the material is bilingual. In one locality, information is available in several languages. Only one county has information designed for use by the visually impaired.

Representations and Complaints

3.42   The Act requires local authorities to establish an effective and accessible procedure for handling complaints and other representations made by children, parents and others in relation to the authority's statutory childcare obligations. Voluntary organisations and registered children's homes are also required to set up similar procedures to consider complaints and other representations made by or on behalf of children accommodated by them but not looked after by local authorities.

3.43   The procedure required by Regulations is a two stage process with a separate independent element at each stage. Local authorities are required to publicise their procedure, and guidance[7] makes it clear that this should be done widely and in an accessible manner.

3.44   The national monitoring survey revealed that every local authority area had established a representations and complaints source. Five authorities had failed so far to take steps to publicise their complaints services. The remaining authorities were publicising their procedures in a variety of ways. These included roadshows and audio or video tapes. Other authorities produced media articles and booklets or gave talks to local groups. User/carer publicity was most commonly available in the form of leaflets, obtainable in service points eg libraries, GP surgeries, council offices.

[7]   The Children Act 1989 Guidance and Regulations Volume 3: Family Placements, Chapter 10: Representations Procedure.

3.45   In 48 authorities material was made available in languages other than English and 41 in ways which take account of the needs of those with sensory or other disabilities. Not all of these authorities did both; as shown in figure 3.2.

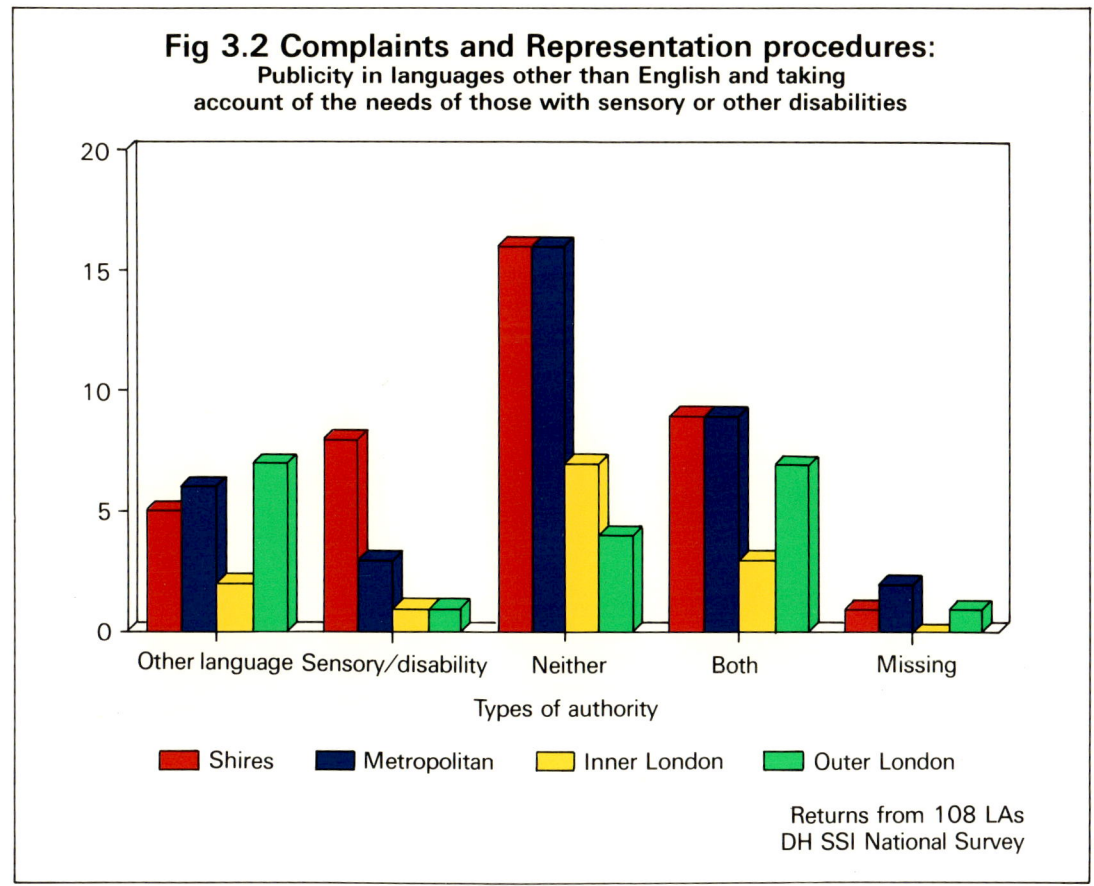

Fig 3.2 Complaints and Representation procedures:
Publicity in languages other than English and taking
account of the needs of those with sensory or other disabilities

Types of authority

■ Shires   ■ Metropolitan   □ Inner London   ■ Outer London

Returns from 108 LAs
DH SSI National Survey

3.46   As with the publicity for the provision of services to children in need, it is to be expected that, in some authorities, the absence of a sizeable minority ethnic population might explain the lack of material in languages other than English. However, as all areas are likely to include children with disabilities, the production of material taking account of their needs by only 34 authorities in the case of provision of services and 41 authorities with respect to complaints procedures is disappointing and suggests a need for some authorities to re-examine their equal opportunities policy.

Designated complaints officer

3.47   Policy guidance recommends that an officer be designated to take day to day responsibility for coordination of the procedure and that the post should be of a sufficiently senior level to reflect the importance of the task and the authority's commitment to it.

3.48   Only one authority at the time of the national monitoring survey, had yet to appoint a designated complaints officer. Of the other 107 authorities, it is encouraging to note that those officers appointed were based apart from the direct line of service provision (for example in the Inspection Unit) and that the posts were graded at a satisfactorily high level. Results also indicated that designated complaints officers were receiving appropriate senior management support.

Numbers of complaints received

3.49   Authorities were asked how many complaints they had received between 14 October 1991 and 30 June 1992 and, of these, how many had been made by children on their own behalf. Table 3.12 shows a wide variation in the numbers recorded and, of those authorities reporting large numbers, few were received from children.

TABLE 3.12   Complaints received grouped by type of authority

	Total	Range per LA	Total from children	Range per LA
Shire county	2,347	0–290	218	0–32
Metropolitan district	987	0–281	241	0–44
Inner London	129	0– 39	38	0–13
Outer London	347	2–152	45	0– 9
Nationally	3,810	0–291	542	0–44

Source: DH SSI national survey   No. of returns = 108

3.50   Reasons for this variation across authorities are not clear but it is likely that different criteria apply and that systems for registration may not be comparable. Local authorities have expressed some confusion as to the distinction between a formal complaint and the every day interaction that takes place between social service staff and their clients. Further definition may be needed on what should be recorded as a complaint. In the early months after the Act was implemented, SSI mounted a series of seminars in English regions to develop understanding of these issues. The Department of Health with SSI will monitor this situation to determine whether further development work, inspections and guidance are needed.

Independent Persons

3.51   The role of the independent person in the complaints process is not to act as advocate for the child nor as investigator but to provide an objective element in the responsible authority's consideration of the complaint. Table 3.13 suggests that many authorities are setting up contracts with children's organisations to provide independent persons for this purpose. In 75 of the 107 responding authorities independent persons were appointed from the voluntary sector and 25 authorities appointed from guardian *ad litem*panels. Other sources of recruitment were retired professionals, academics and those with a legal background.

TABLE 3.13   Source of independent persons

	Number of LAs
Employee of other LA	17
Member of other LA	4
Health authority	13
Voluntary sector	75
Specialist advocacy service	32
GAL panel	25
Other	54

Source: DH SSI national survey   No. of returns = 107

3.52   Additional information gleaned from the SSI national workshops on complaints revealed:

(i) *Support for Complainants*

90 authorities are making some form of support provision to assist clients in using the system and pursuing their complaint through the procedure. The definition of "support" is being widely interpreted. Support may be needed for example to assist those with learning disabilities, or sensory disabilities; others whose first language is not English may need help in communicating these concerns. Young children in particular may need the help of a suitable, friendly and independent adult to help them.

(ii) *Time Limits*

The majority of authorities complied with the time limits for handling complaints. Some had introduced shorter ones, or planned to do so. Some considered the time limits to be impracticable for complex cases and this was exacerbated where there were staffing problems.

Wales

3.53 All respondent authorities in Wales have a complaints procedure in place and 7 out of 8 had a designated complaints officer. 11 complaints were dealt with formally which specifically related to children. The existence of the complaints procedure was widely publicised. All provided for an independent person to be involved, usually Guardians ad Litem, but voluntary sector appointments were made in one case; in another independent persons were recruited by newspaper advertisement and came from various backgrounds.

Chapter 4: Day Care for Under-Eights and Review Duty

Background

4.1 Most children attending day nurseries or being looked after by childminders do so through private arrangements made by their parents with those who provide the services. The Children Act gives local authorities a duty to regulate these services to ensure acceptable standards in the interests of children's welfare and safety and reassurance for parents. Additionally, through their local child care plans, which will be produced after conducting the review of day care services, authorities are to encourage a coherent and sensible expansion of services.

4.2 In the first twelve months since implementation local authorities had to re-register existing day care providers and childminders, apply the new legislation and guidance to new services and carry out the first review of the pattern of provision in their areas.

4.3 The national monitoring survey sought information from local authorities on:

● the re-registration exercise

● their ability to meet the recommended time-limits for processing applications for registration from intending childminders and providers of day care

● compliance with recommended staff/child ratios

● mechanisms used to conduct the first review of day care services.

4.4 In drawing conclusions around local authority performance in these key tasks it is necessary to sound a general note of caution. The largest numbers of incomplete responses to the survey were received on the day care section. In assessing progress it has been assumed that those who failed to respond were also having difficulties in meeting their targets but this may not necessarily be so. Secondly, the survey asked for information as at 30 June 1992. Action taken since then sought to ensure that those authorities giving cause for concern have taken the necessary steps to improve performance.

Re-registration of Existing Services

4.5 Under the transitional provisions in the Act childminders and people providing day-care services on non-domestic premises, who had been registered under the Nurseries and Childminders Regulation Act 1948, had to be re-registered under the new legislation within 12 months of the Act coming into force, that is, the exercise had to be completed by no later than 13 October 1992.

4.6 At the end of June some 52 or about 50% of local authorities in England—5 Inner London authorities, 11 Outer London authorities, 15 Metropolitan authorities and 21 Shire authorities—had made little progress with re-registration. This meant that through no fault of their own childminders and day-care providers who had not been re-registered would be acting unlawfully if they continued to provide a service. The Department warned these 52 authorities about the implications of this failure and 47 reported subsequently that they had either met the 13 October deadline or would complete the exercise within a few weeks.

4.7 Five authorities reported that it would take some months to complete the registration process. The reasons these 5 authorities gave for being unable to meet the due date included:

● time taken to recruit and appoint additional staff to improve the registration system;

● no extra resources available in 1992/93;

● industrial action by social services staff.

4.8   The Department is now monitoring the progress being made in each of the five authorities. Ministers have also written to one authority to express their concern about the situation.

Time Limits for Processing New Registrations.

4.9   In Volume 2 in the Children Act guidance series the Department introduced recommended time limits within which local authorities should aim to complete the registration process. The limits set were:

- 3 months for intending childminders and providers of sessional day care (ie play groups and out of schools clubs)

- 6 months for intending full day care providers (ie day nurseries and all day holiday play-schemes)[1].

4.10   The information supplied in answer to the questionnaire represented the position after the Act had been in force just under nine months, during which local authorities had also been working on re-registering existing childminders and day-care providers. It would be premature at this stage to draw firm conclusions about the effectiveness of these recommended limits on the efficiency or speed of the registration system but first impressions suggest the time limits were not impossible to meet. Many authorities, however, will need to look to their registration procedures and continue to find ways of improving their performance.

4.11   Figures 4.1–4.5 provide some indications about the differences in registration performance between types of local authority in England by type of day care service for those authorities who had received applications as at 30 June 1992. In interpreting the findings consideration must be given to the range of applications received for the different services. These showed considerable variation between types of authority but was particularly marked for sessional day care services and childminders. There was no obvious relationship between workload and completion rates—low numbers of applications did not guarantee 100% completion within the recommended time limits.

4.12   Of the 84% of authorities that responded all reported receiving applications from new **childminders**. Fig 4.1 shows that only 11 authorities were able to process all applications within the recommended time limits whilst a further 23 were able to process none within the deadline.

---

[1]   The survey provided information on the ability of local authorities to complete the registration process for sessional services for under 5s within **six** months of receipt. This allows for comparison between full day care services and sessional services.

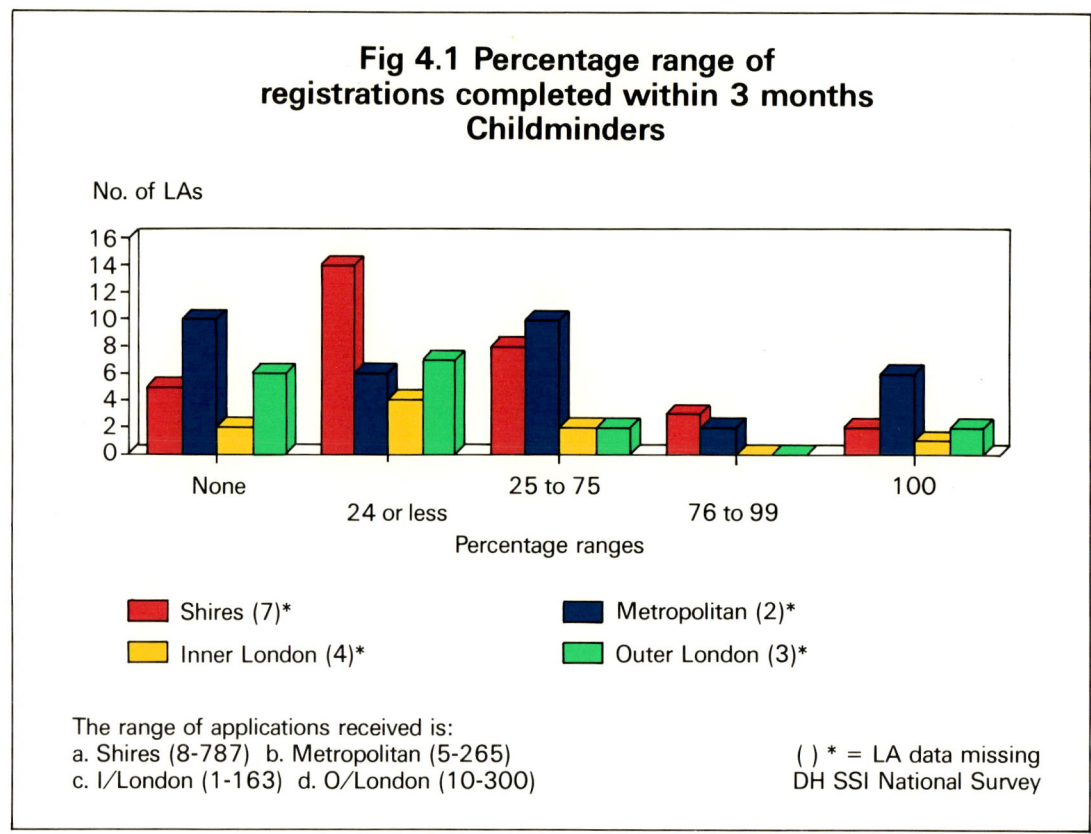

Fig 4.1 Percentage range of registrations completed within 3 months Childminders

No. of LAs

Percentage ranges

Shires (7)*   Metropolitan (2)*
Inner London (4)*   Outer London (3)*

The range of applications received is:
a. Shires (8-787) b. Metropolitan (5-265)
c. I/London (1-163) d. O/London (10-300)

( ) * = LA data missing
DH SSI National Survey

4.13   The volume of applications for new **day nurseries** was far lower than those for childminders. The questionnaire returns covered 80% of all local authorities but the number of authorities which handled large numbers of applications was small. 10 local authorities reported receiving no new applications whilst 14 reported receiving more than 10 each. This is to be expected as there are many more registered childminders than day nurseries. Fig 4.2 shows that rather more authorities (27) were able to complete the registration process within the time limits, although the pattern of performance varied by type of authority, particularly for Inner London.

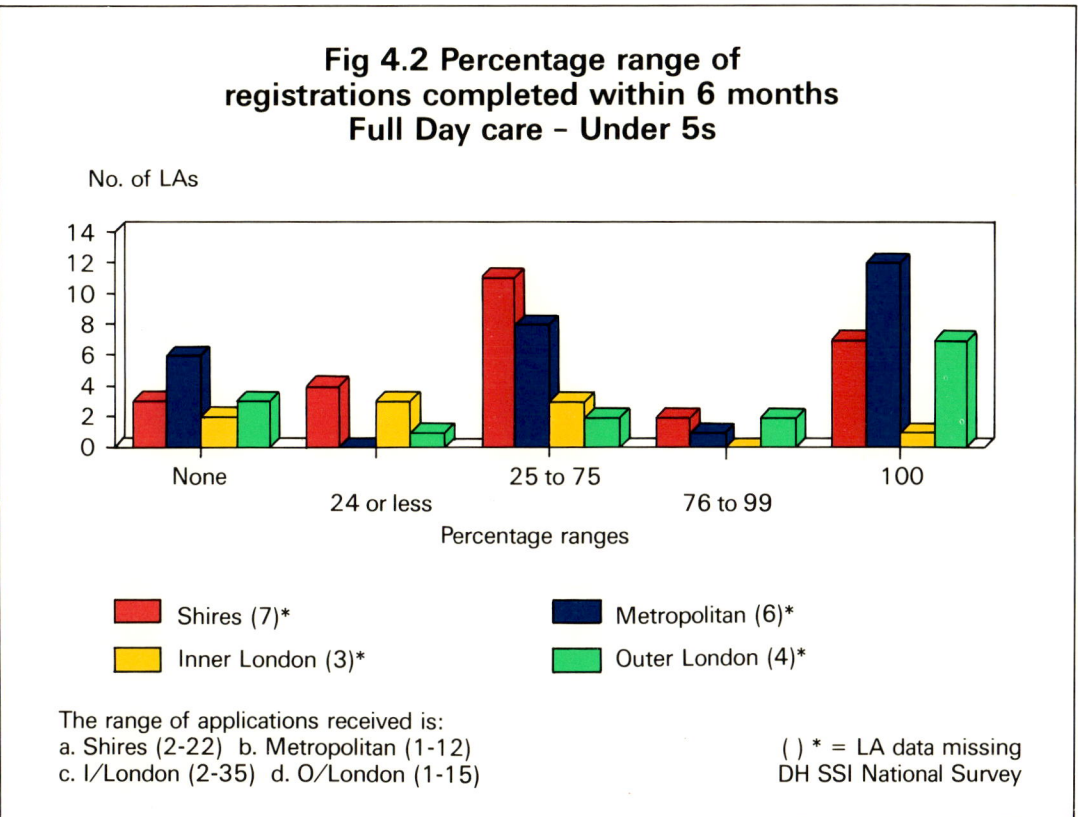

Fig 4.2 Percentage range of registrations completed within 6 months Full Day care – Under 5s

No. of LAs

Percentage ranges

- Shires (7)*
- Metropolitan (6)*
- Inner London (3)*
- Outer London (4)*

The range of applications received is:
a. Shires (2-22)   b. Metropolitan (1-12)
c. I/London (2-35)   d. O/London (1-15)

( ) * = LA data missing
DH SSI National Survey

4.14   The majority of responses showed that authorities had received no new applications from providers of **full day care for 5–7 year olds.** This term covers holiday play schemes and it is likely that many more schemes are organised during the summer holidays (that is, after the date of the monitoring survey) than at other times of the year. The patchy response also reflects the fact that some local authorities have a history of facilitating the setting up of such services, whereas others have not seen it as a priority.

4.15   The survey information reveals that 42 of the responding authorities received no applications and only 13 reported receiving more than 10 applications. It is encouraging to note, however, that the majority were able to register those schemes (many facilitated by the authorities themselves) within the time limits (figure 4.3).

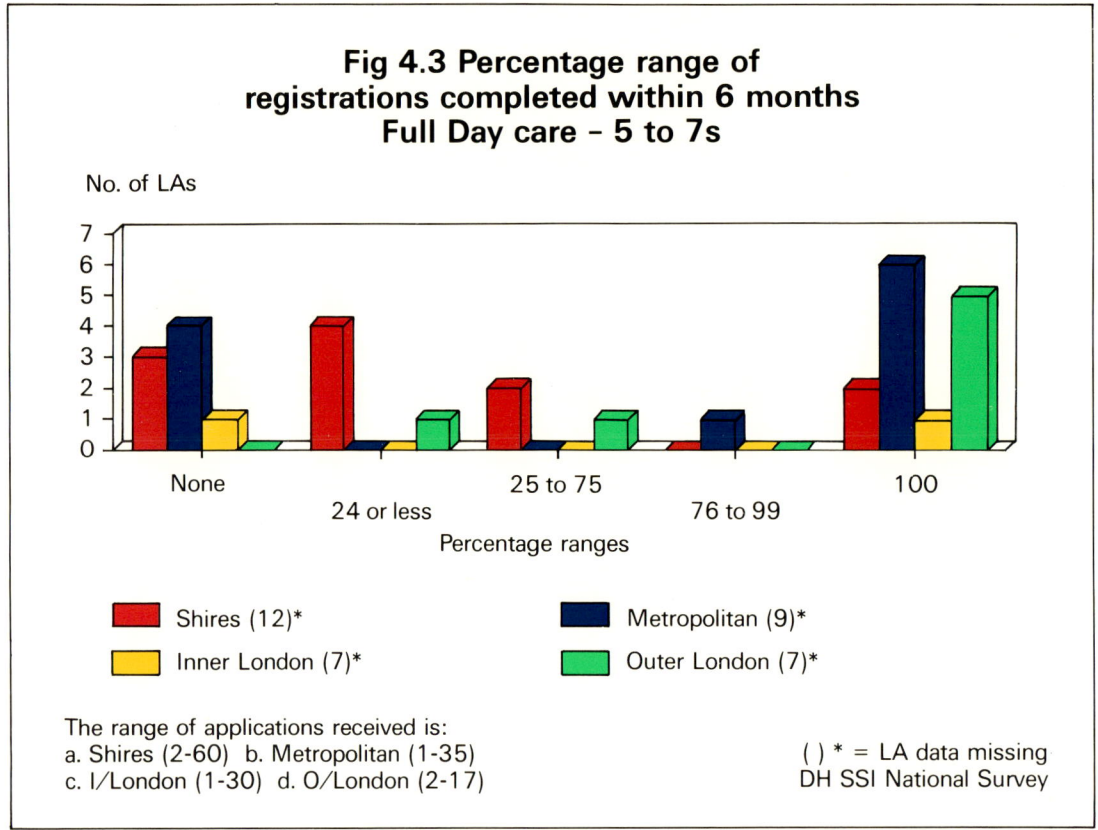

Fig 4.3 Percentage range of registrations completed within 6 months Full Day care – 5 to 7s

4.16 The extent to which authorities have received and processed applications for registration of 'supervised activities' or sessional care for pre-school children and those aged 5–7 years is patchy.

4.17 Although 13% of responding authorities received no applications for **sessional day care for under 5s**, shire counties and to a lesser extent Inner London authorities received significantly more applications than the Metropolitan and Outer London authorities. Two shire county authorities receiving high numbers of applications were able to process all of them within the time limit, which is encouraging. On the other hand Inner London fared less well when authorities receiving high numbers of applications were considered (figure 4.4).

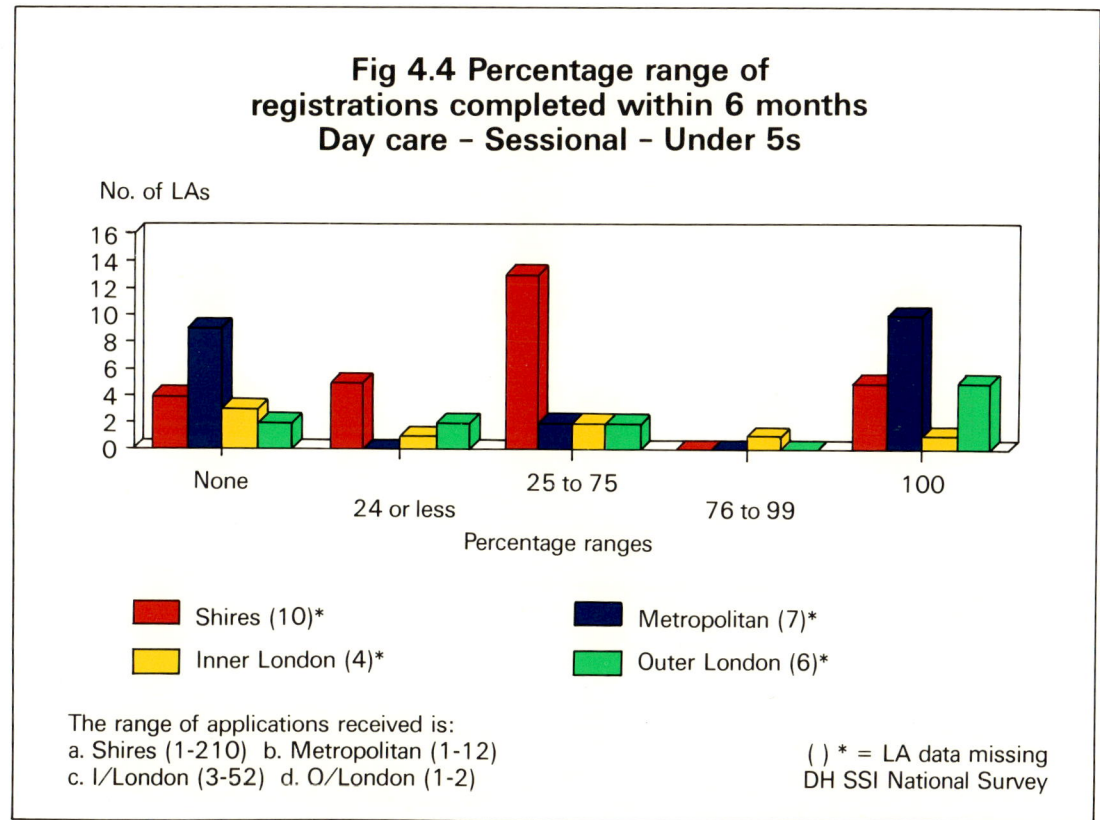

**Fig 4.4 Percentage range of
registrations completed within 6 months
Day care – Sessional – Under 5s**

No. of LAs

Percentage ranges

- Shires (10)*
- Metropolitan (7)*
- Inner London (4)*
- Outer London (6)*

The range of applications received is:
a. Shires (1-210) b. Metropolitan (1-12)
c. I/London (3-52) d. O/London (1-2)

( ) * = LA data missing
DH SSI National Survey

4.18   The pattern of applications by type of authority for **sessional care for 5–7 year olds,** which includes out of school clubs organised during term time, is the reverse of that reported for under 5s. 37 authorities reported receiving no applications, and this, taken with the numbers of incomplete returns, means that the available information on completed registrations covers less than 34% of the country (figure 4.5).

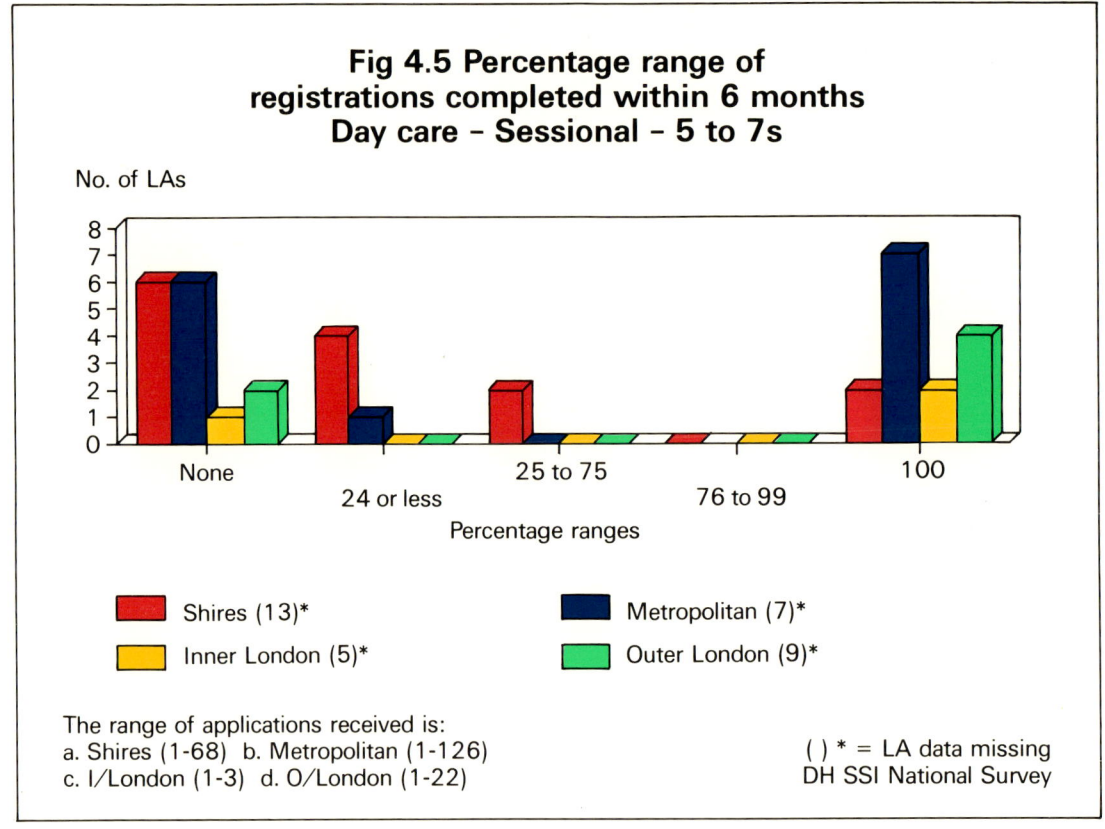

Fig 4.5 Percentage range of
registrations completed within 6 months
Day care – Sessional – 5 to 7s

Wales

4.19   The survey returns submitted by local authorities in Wales have not been fully analysed. There were significant inconsistencies in the way the information contained in the returns had been collated. Most local authorities expected to complete re-registration of those providing childminding and day care services in non-domestic premises by 13 October 1992. The position with new registrations is more varied across Wales but authorities were expecting to be on schedule by October 1992.

Staff/Child Ratios

4.20   The Department made recommendations about the appropriate staff/child ratios after wide-ranging consultation. The ratios recommended in Volume 2 allow providers to offer acceptable standards of care for children and affordable services. The Department has undertaken to review the ratios after the Act has been in force for 2 years. The questionnaire survey sought information on the proportion of local authorities using the recommended ratios, and to find out what different ones, if any, were being applied.

4.21   The recommended ratios are set out below:

Full Day Care

Age Range	Ratio
0–2	1:3
2–3	1:4
3–5	1:8
5–7	1:8

Sessional Day Care

Age Range	Ratio
3–5	1:8
5–7	1:8

Childminding

Age Range	Ratio
0–5	1:3
5–7	1:6
0–8	1:6—with not more than 3 aged under 5

4.22   Overall 56% of the 107 responding authorities were using the ratios as recommended in the guidance, but there were differences between the types of authority as shown in figures 4.6 – 4.8. In shire counties the proportion was 62%, in metropolitan authorities 53%, in inner London 46% and in outer London 58%. No authority reported using different ratios for all types of setting.

4.23   Figure 4.6 shows that a very high proportion of authorities were using the recommended ratios for **childminders** and that there was little variation across the age groups. Where other ratios have been adopted these were lower than recommended (that is more children to childminders) and were confined primarily to a few shire and metropolitan authorities in the 5–7 and 0–8 range.

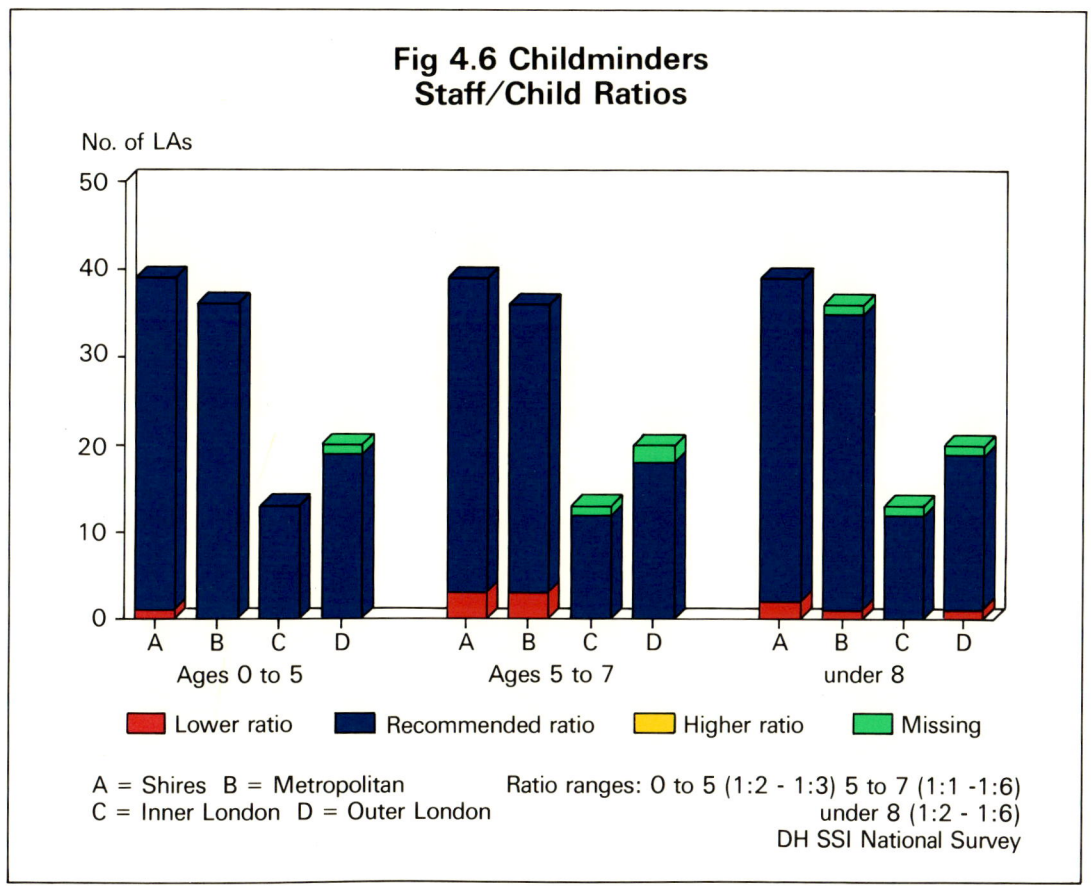

4.24   For **full day care** the variation in ratios was more marked particularly for the 2–3 and 3–5 age groups and applied across all types of authority (figure 4.7). 26 applied higher ratios (that is fewer children to staff) for the 3–5 age group. For the 2–3 age group 4 authorities have adopted higher ratios and 17 authorities have adopted lower ratios.

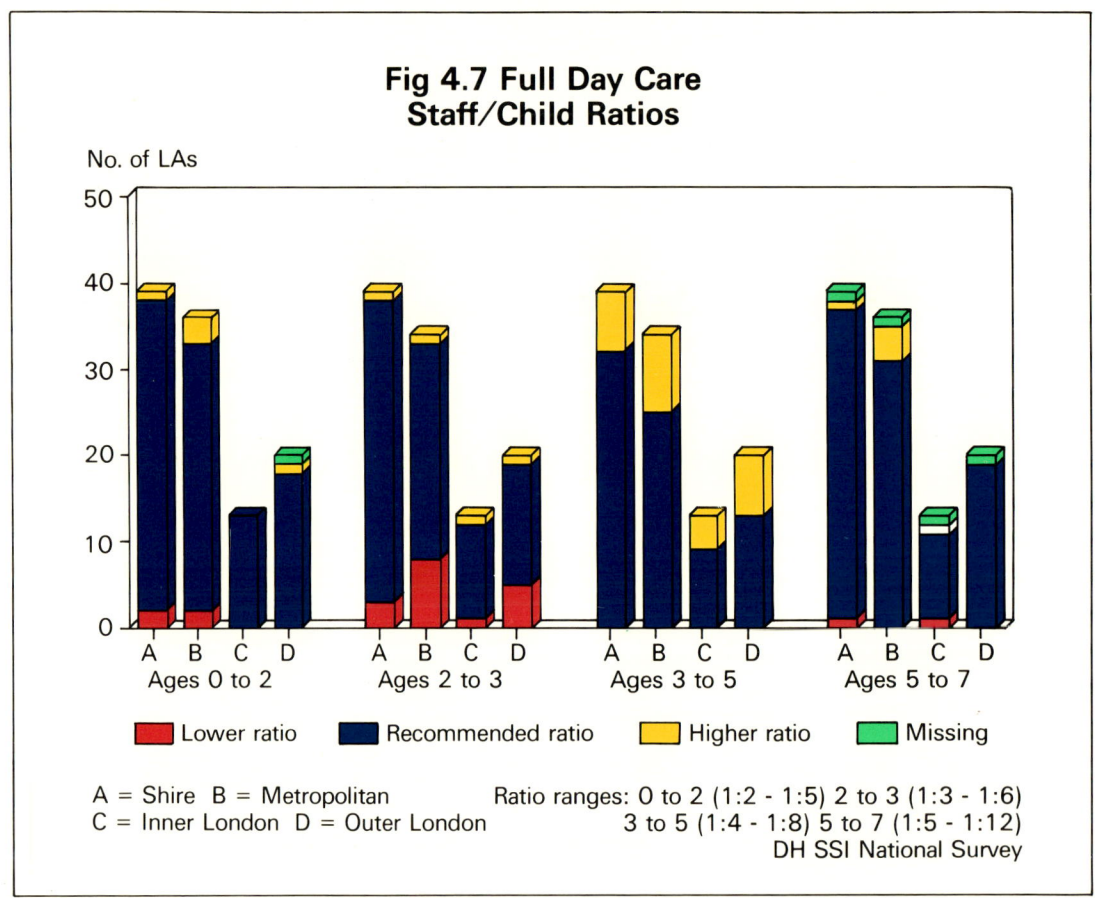

4.25   Figure 4.8 suggests greater uniformity in the use of recommended ratios for **sessional day care** although a larger number of shire authorities reported using higher ratios for 3–5 year olds.

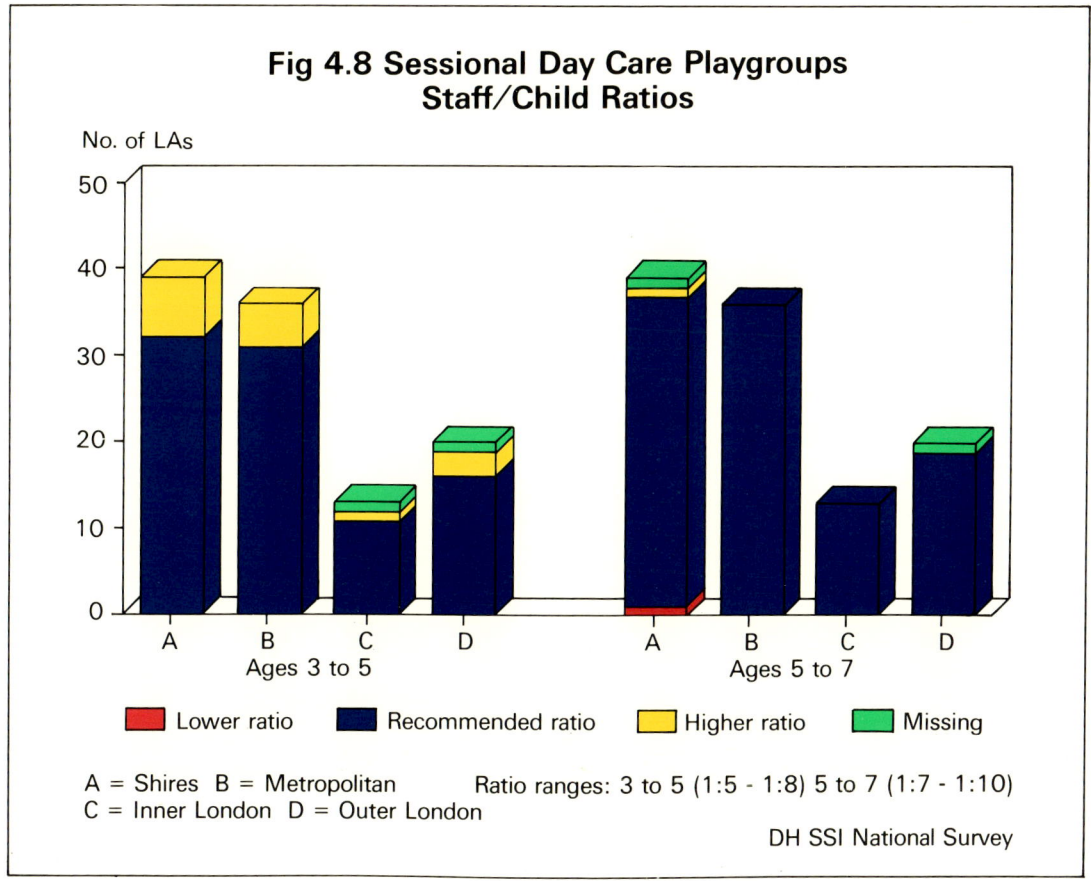

**Fig 4.8 Sessional Day Care Playgroups
Staff/Child Ratios**

No. of LAs

Legend: Lower ratio | Recommended ratio | Higher ratio | Missing

A = Shires B = Metropolitan   Ratio ranges: 3 to 5 (1:5 - 1:8) 5 to 7 (1:7 - 1:10)
C = Inner London D = Outer London

DH SSI National Survey

Wales

4.26   Seven local authorities in Wales used the recommended ratios for sessional day care and childminders. For the authorities that differed, one used a slightly higher staff to child ratio for sessional day care but also used slightly different age-bands; the other used a slightly lower childminder to child ratio in the 0–5 age band. In full day care settings five local authorities used the recommended ratios. Where there was a difference but comparable age-bands a lower staff to child ratio was adopted in the 2–3 age group.

Review Duty

4.27   This new duty, under which social services departments and local education authorities are required to review the day care services in their area and publish a report every three years gives local authorities a strategic function for these services for the first time. This provides an effective mechanism for ensuring coherent and sensible expansion of day care services. Local authorities are required to complete the first reviews within twelve months of the Act coming into force.

4.28   To assist in this process the Department of Health is funding a three year project based in the Early Childhood Unit of the National Children's Bureau to evaluate the review. The project will analyse the reports of the first review to produce guidelines for good practice to assist authorities with the next review due to be conducted in 1995. The outcome of the first review will form a topic for discussion in next year's Children Act report.

4.29 The national monitoring survey sought information as at 30 June about the mechanisms being used by local authorities to undertake the review duty. These are illustrated in figure 4.9.

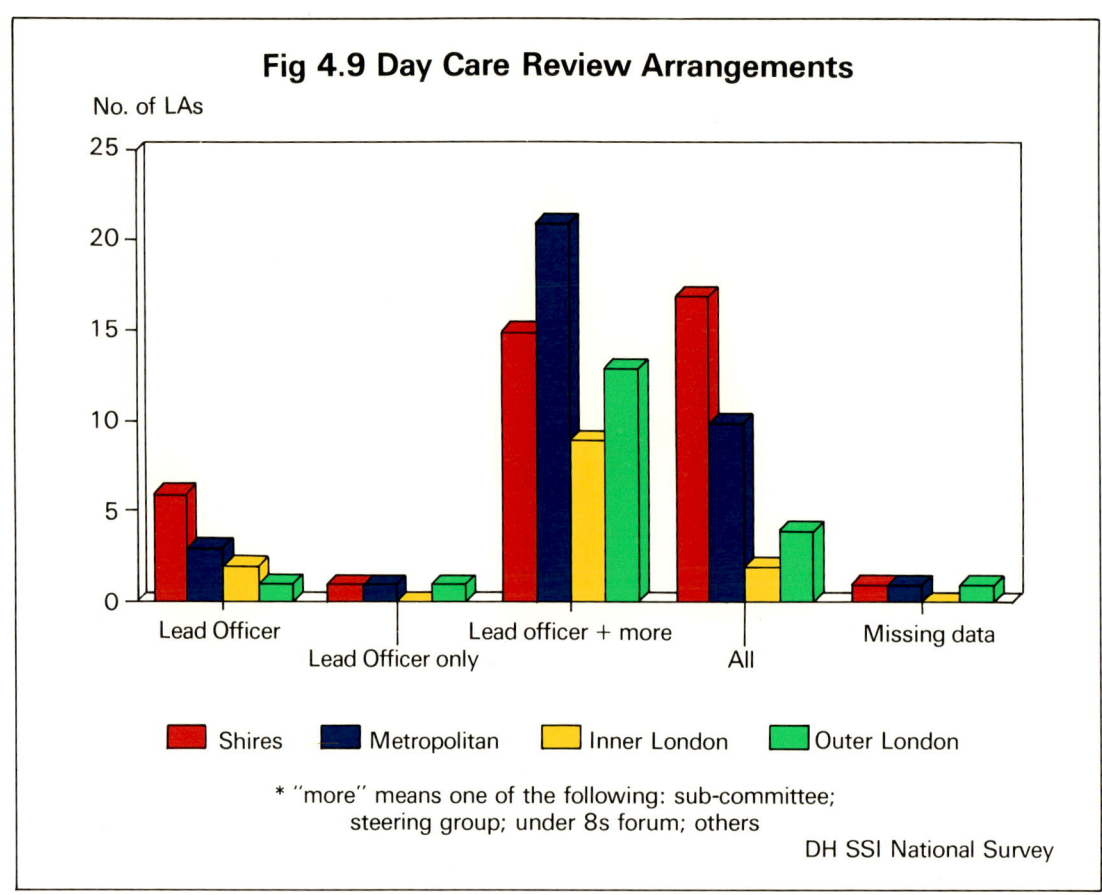

Fig 4.9 Day Care Review Arrangements

No. of LAs

* "more" means one of the following: sub-committee; steering group; under 8s forum; others

Shires   Metropolitan   Inner London   Outer London

DH SSI National Survey

4.30 Nearly every authority recognised that the work involved in carrying out the review duty needed to have a focal point at officer level and 89% of authorities have appointed a lead officer. The majority had also set up steering groups but a significant number had failed to involve local elected members through a member level committee to oversee the review.

4.31 Although the Act does not require local authorities to consult relevant organisations during the review process, the Department urges them to do this. It is therefore of concern that just one third of authorities had so far failed to set up an under 8s forum which would have provided a useful vehicle for consulting widely and regularly within the voluntary and independent sectors in particular.

4.32 Figure 4.9 shows that 58 authorities had appointed a lead officer and had established at least a steering committee, member sub-committee or under 8s forum. Of those authorities reporting that they had none of these mechanisms in place, two metropolitan authorities said they had established other arrangements. Altogether 42 authorities reported using other arrangements which included ad hoc consultation with education, leisure and housing departments, the health service and the voluntary and private sectors.

4.33 In Wales six authorities had appointed a lead officer in addition to either at least a sub-committee of members, a steering group or had established a local forum. Two authorities had in place all four arrangements. Other agencies reported to be involved in the Review duty included education departments, health authorities, voluntary and private sector.

Further Guidance on Day Care

4.34   The findings from the national survey on progress in implementing the day care provisions of the Act—particularly around registration of providers and staff/ child ratios—reinforced a general concern that a significant number of local authorities were not using the legislation and guidance constructively.

4.35   Examination of correspondence from MPs and the general public confirmed that some local authorities were seeking to impose on childminders and daycare providers more stringent or higher standards than those recommended in the national guidance. Some local authorities appeared to have adopted an over-rigid approach to registration of existing provision. As a result many daycare providers and childminders were finding it difficult and onerous to comply with the registration requirements imposed by local authorities.

4.36   The aspects giving rise to particular difficulties were: application of space standards and staff/child ratios; availability of separate sanitary facilities in day nurseries; proportion of trained staff; registration requirements for people providing playgroups on domestic premises; legislation on food safety and fire safety; first aid; health checks on applicants; criminal record checks; definition of supervised activities; day care services on NHS premises and those covered by Crown immunity.

4.37   The Department, whilst recognising local authorities' statutory responsibility for application of standards in individual cases, decided to issue a circular so as to ensure that the general approach to registration did not inhibit expansion of good quality day care services and childminding.

4.38   The circular (which was published on 11 January), reminds authorities that, in the interests of children and families they must strike the right balance between ensuring standards and encouraging development of provision. There is a presumption under the legislation that registration should be granted unless the authority has good reason not to register. Authorities need to ensure that their registration procedures operate promptly and should not apply the Department's guidance over-rigidly or set standards higher than those recommended by the Department without good reason. The Department is confident that the circular will assist local authorities to adopt a more constructive approach to regulation.

Chapter 5: Residential Child Care

Background

5.1 The effect of the Children Act 1989 in respect of local authority community homes for children and voluntary children's homes was largely to consolidate the earlier legislation of 1948 and 1980. A new provision was made, however, to require private children's homes to be registered by the local authority.

5.2 Implementation of the Act presented the opportunity to provide up to date Regulations and guidance to replace earlier Regulations framed in 1951 in respect of voluntary homes and in 1972 in respect of community homes. There have been many changes in patterns of child care since the earlier Regulations were drafted and the Children's Homes Regulations 1991 reflect these. (The total number of children in care in England fell from a peak of nearly 100,000 to under 60,000 just prior to implementation; the proportion of children in residential care had fallen compared with those in foster care; children in care living in residential care tend now to represent the older age range and often have complex problems to surmount.)

5.3 The new Regulations and guidance were published in Volume 4 of the series of Children Act Guidance and Regulations ("Residential Care"). This volume reflects the principles and general requirements of the Act. In particular it requires responsible authorities to safeguard and promote the welfare of children living in community homes and children's homes. Due regard must be paid to the wishes and feelings of the children; contact between the children and members of their family, friends and neighbourhoods must be sustained where this is helpful. Particular attention must be paid to encouraging the participation of parents and the exercise of their parental responsibilities.

Utting Report

5.4 In the months prior to implementation of the Act in 1991 the Department of Health received copies of a report commissioned by Staffordshire County Council; this was prepared by Mr Allan Levy and Mrs Barbara Kahan following their enquiry into the "Pindown Experience"[1]. Government's response was to order a review of residential child care by Sir William Utting, then Chief Inspector of the Social Services Inspectorate[2].

5.5 In his report, in August 1991, Sir William recommended that local authorities should draw up plans for child care services giving due weight to residential care; that management techniques should be introduced to residential care services and personnel management policies should encourage people to enter and stay in residential child care; there should be investment in training of, and qualifying courses for, the residential child care workforce; and that local authority children's homes should be inspected by authorities' 'arms length' inspection units. The Department accepted the thrust of the recommendations and has set up a Joint Utting Implementation Group (JUIG) involving local authority, voluntary and training interests.

5.6 Sir William also recommended that the Secretary of State should consider making periodic public reports of progress in implementing the Children Act and that the Department of Health should report in 18 months time to the Secretary of State on the first year's operation of the Regulations and Guidance and institute further monitoring if desirable. This report provides a response to those recommendations.

5.7 The work of JUIG is under way and action has already been taken on a number of issues:

   (1) A residential child care training initiative has been mounted to enable Heads and Deputy Heads of children's homes, and other homes staff with management potential, to be trained to qualifying standards. A total of 422 staff are currently undergoing this training.

---

[1] The Pindown Experience and the Protection of Children: The Report of the Staffordshire Child Care Inquiry, published May 1991.

[2] Children in the Public Care—A Review of Residential Child Care published by the Department of Health, August 1991.

(2) An expert group has examined the residential childcare content of qualifying training courses and has assisted the Central Council for Education and Training in Social Work to produce guidance to Diploma in Social Work programmes about the teaching of residential child-care.

(3) The Department of Health has drafted further guidance to supplement that in Volume 4 on issues of control and restraint. The draft guidance has been issued for consultation to the Local Authority Associations, voluntary organisations and professional bodies and is being debated vigorously. A circular issued under Ministerial guidance will be issued shortly.

(4) A circular has been issued to authorities asking them to inspect local authority and private children's homes using their "arms-length" inspection unit. The circular provides advice about frequency of inspection, methodology, standards and staffing of inspection teams.

(5) A further circular asks authorities to implement Sir William Utting's recommendation that they should prepare and keep plans for all children's services provided by the authority, including residential care. This will encourage authorities to make explicit their policies, to recognise resource implications and ensure that resource allocation reflects these policies. Local authorities will also have to make clear the gaps they wish to see filled by the voluntary and private sector. The circular provides guidance on the content of children's services plans and asks that these should pay particular attention in the first year to defining a positive role for residential care recognising the strategic importance of the residential sector and ensuring that its use is consistent with that role.

(6) The Department of Health is discussing with the Department for Education the question of guidance to education authorities about the educational needs of children being looked after by local authorities.

(7) The Joint Utting Implementation Group has been investigating issues of whether regulatory procedures affecting children in residential placements other than in children's homes are suitable.

(8) In addition the Local Authority Associations are, at the request of the Joint Utting Implementation Group preparing guidance on the role of authority members in relation to children being looked after by the authority.

(9) As a result of the concerns over standards of care in children's homes, the National Joint Council for Local Authorities Administrative, Professional, Technical and Clerical Services established in 1991 a Joint Inquiry into local authority residential staffs pay and terms and conditions of service, and various other management issues. The inquiry was chaired by Lady Howe and her report has been presented and published.

(10) One crucial issue identified by Sir William Utting was that of the suitability of staff employed and the methods used in their selection and appointment. This reflects concerns raised in Leicestershire surrounding the conviction in 1991 of Frank Beck and others. The Warner Report, published on 7 December 1992 dealt with these concerns and with other issues relevant to the protection of young children, and to the support and guidance of staff in children's homes. The Report was critical of personnel procedures and methods of selection and recruitment of staff and of the absence of plans for suitable staff appraisal. It made recommendations on training, a licensing system for residential care workers, a code of practice setting national standards, better monitoring, improved vetting, better supervision of staff and improved arrangements for the vetting of staff by the police. Local authorities were asked to respond to the key recommendations on personnel practices and the selection and appointments of staff and to report back on progress by April 1993. The outcome of that process and other issues taken forward arising from Warner will feature in next year's Children Act report.

Wales

5.8 The Social Services Inspectorate undertook a review of local authority, voluntary and private children's homes. A report, 'Accommodating Children' was published in January 1992. The review differed somewhat from that of Sir William Utting in that direct interviews took place with social services managers in all 8 Welsh authorities; a third of all homes were visited and care staff and children were interviewed. The review made a number of recommendations. Principal among these were that homes should form an integral part of local authority child care strategies, that analysis needs to take place of urgent and unplanned admissions in each authority and that children who present 'seriously challenging behaviour' should be accommodated within dedicated provision. Consideration is being given to the means by which to take forward the recommendations of this review.

Implementation of Children's Homes Regulations and Section 63

5.9 Within a series of recommendations, Sir William Utting recommended (in August 1991) that:

> "22.3 (the) Department of Health report in 18 months time to the Secretary of State on the first year's operation of the Regulations and Guidance (Vol. 4) and institute further monitoring if desirable."

The national survey conducted in June 1992 contributed to the fulfilment of this recommendation. The survey sought information from authorities on a selection of issues typical of the whole and from which some judgement of progress towards implementation could be drawn. Responses to the survey are recorded as follows.

5.10 Of the 108 English authorities responding to this part of the survey, 6 reported that they were not responsible for the management of any community homes. Of the remainder, the average number of homes managed averaged over 9 per authority.

Statements of Purpose and Function

5.11 Regulation 4 of the Children's Homes Regulations 1991 requires local authorities to have produced by 14 January 1992 a written statement including the purpose of the home and various other particulars. The statement should describe what the home sets out to do for children and the manner in which care is provided. It is intended to be directed at those making placements, and for those working in the home and responsible for it as well as parents and children. The production and maintenance of this statement is a crucial requirement as so much stems from an agreed understanding of the purpose and objectives of homes.

5.12 The survey revealed that by June 1992 just over one half of all authorities had produced these statements for all of their homes. A further one-fifth of all authorities had met this requirement in part. A number of large authorities with well above the average number of homes have yet to complete the task but appear to be working on it. It is of considerable concern, however, that eighteen authorities appeared to have taken no action whatsoever on this requirement. This raises the question of whether these authorities have sound strategies for child care generally and for residential child care in particular.

Staff Supervision

5.13 Staff in children's community homes require supervision in order to receive advice and emotional support in what is a demanding occupation; supervision also provides a means of achieving accountability.

5.14 Guidance advises that all staff working in children's homes should receive individual supervision from their line manager. Care staff should ideally receive supervision for one to one and a half hours not less frequently than once every two to three weeks. Other staff should be seen just as frequently but the length of each session would not normally need to be so long.

5.15 The response to the survey showed that 94 local authorities roughly complied with the Guidance by requiring supervision for more than one hour fortnightly to monthly. However, the questionnaire assumed uniformity of practice within a local authority for all their community homes. This was evidently not the case as some local authorities which reported to be complying with this aspect of the guidance also reported less frequent supervision in some homes. Thus, a further 38 responses reported supervision at the same frequency but for only up to one hour. 7 authorities did not require supervision at all and a few authorities required supervision less than monthly.

5.16 The survey results indicate that authorities in general expect to be able to comply with the Guidance in Volume 4 on standards of supervision of staff. SSI will include this standard in its format of inspection criteria currently being developed.

Guidance to Staff in Residential Homes

5.17 Guidance advises local authorities that they should issue written guidance on important procedures to staff. The survey contained questions designed to see how far local authorities were supporting residential child care staff by writing guidance on a number of specific issues directly related to practice within children's homes. Over a quarter of authorities with homes claimed to have issued guidance on each of the topics cited. Of those authorities which responded the survey showed:

- 78 authorities had issued guidance on *log book and diary recording* whilst 25 had not issued this guidance.

- 65 authorities had issued guidance on arrangements for *regulating and vetting visitors* to the home whilst 37 had not.

- 39 had issued guidance to staff on care practices when working with *children of the opposite sex* whilst 62 had not.

- 84 had issued guidance on dealing with *aggression and violence whilst 19 had not.*

- 62 had issued guidance on *Working with Parents* whilst 41 had not.

- 29 authorities had issued guidance on all the topics concerned.

- 8 authorities had issued no guidance and 13 had only issued guidance on one subject.

5.18 The poorest positive response rate to these guidance requirements is in relation to that of staff care practices towards children of the opposite sex. Only about a third of authorities have tackled this issue whereas in relation to other pieces of guidance, the figure is approximately two thirds. This may reflect continuing nervousness and uncertainty in relation to how residential care staff should deal with issues of sexuality.

5.19 Guidance (in Vol. 4) emphasises the importance of staff being alert to the risks of abuse of children in homes. Despite the high degree of public concern over this issue (and the requirement to report abuse, in Regulation 19 of the 1991 Regulations) only 70 authorities had issued guidance to their staff on this topic. This is a matter for concern. It accords with continuing evidence that although the situation is improving, some authorities remain uncertain about how to act when abuse in residential child care is revealed. This seems to be so not withstanding the guidance issued in the "Working Together" document and Volume 4 of the Children Act Guidance.

Approved Sanctions

5.20 Departmental guidance in Vol. 4 advised that local authorities should detail in writing the disciplinary measures which it approves for use in each of its children's homes; the guidance says that other sanctions should not be employed. The Regulations prohibit various measures, including corporal punishment, restrictions on visits, requirements to wear distinctive or inappropriate clothing. (Restriction of liberty is closely regulated under the Secure Accommodation Regulations). 92 authorities replied that they had issued guidance on approved sanctions, 11 said they had not and 5 did not answer the question.

Positive Means of Control

5.21   Guidance advises local authorities to develop written policies for each home aimed at securing the successful conduct of the home through a combination of sound management, high standards of professional practice and care planning and upon caring relationships. 73 authorities said they had produced such a policy document, 30 said they had not and 5 did not answer the question.

5.22   The fact that 30 authorities are content to indicate that they have not addressed this matter seems somewhat surprising, given the high profile of the subject. However the fact that there has not been as much Departmental guidance on the topic as some feel there might have been may provide some explanation for this. Guidance on Control and Restraint in children's homes is in an advanced state of preparation, following consultations with outside interests.

Provision of Telephones

5.23   The new Children's Homes Regulations require authorities to ensure that a pay-phone is available in each home in a setting where it is possible to make and receive calls in privacy. However good child care may be there is nevertheless concern that children become isolated from family members and former associations. The requirement to provide telephones serves to remedy this; it also provides access to known help-lines.

5.24   Less than half of all authorities' homes have complied fully or largely with this new requirement; 41 per cent, however, have less than one quarter of their homes equipped with a pay-phone. This is a surprisingly disappointing response on this question. It raises the question whether the reasons are cost, professional objections, or managerial inactivity. What is worrying is the possibility that this failure to instal telephones may indicate a custodial attitude towards children in residential child care.

Visits on Behalf of the Responsible Authority

5.25   Regulation 22 of the 1991 Regulations, with associated Guidance requires authorities to ensure that children's homes are visited once a month. The person visiting is required to submit a written report to the authority on the conduct of the home. The guidance to local authorities *makes clear that* the visits should not be made by anyone employed at the home. These visits are expected to be made by members of the Social Services Committee of the Council or by an officer who does not have any responsibility in relation to the management, administration or conduct of the home.

5.26   "Member visits" were considered to be of great importance in the Utting Review in demonstrating elected members personal responsibility for the welfare of children in children's homes. It is a mechanism whereby members have some hope of knowing what is going on in homes, and therefore some mechanism for accountability which was so obviously lacking in Staffordshire.

5.27   The survey suggests that just over two fifths of authorities claimed to have carried out all or more of the required number of visits. A few gave responses which indicated confusion about the requirements of the regulation.

5.28 Figure 5.1 shows that nationally 50 (49%) authorities report having achieved 75% or more of the required visits with 38 (37%) of these having achieved 100%. Nine authorities report achieving less than 25% of required visits with just one authority reporting no visits made. When it comes to the completion of written reports of the visits, the picture worsens. Only 17 authorities claim to have completed the full 100% of written reports. 22 authorities claim to have written 25% or less and 6 of those report writing none at all (figure 5.2).

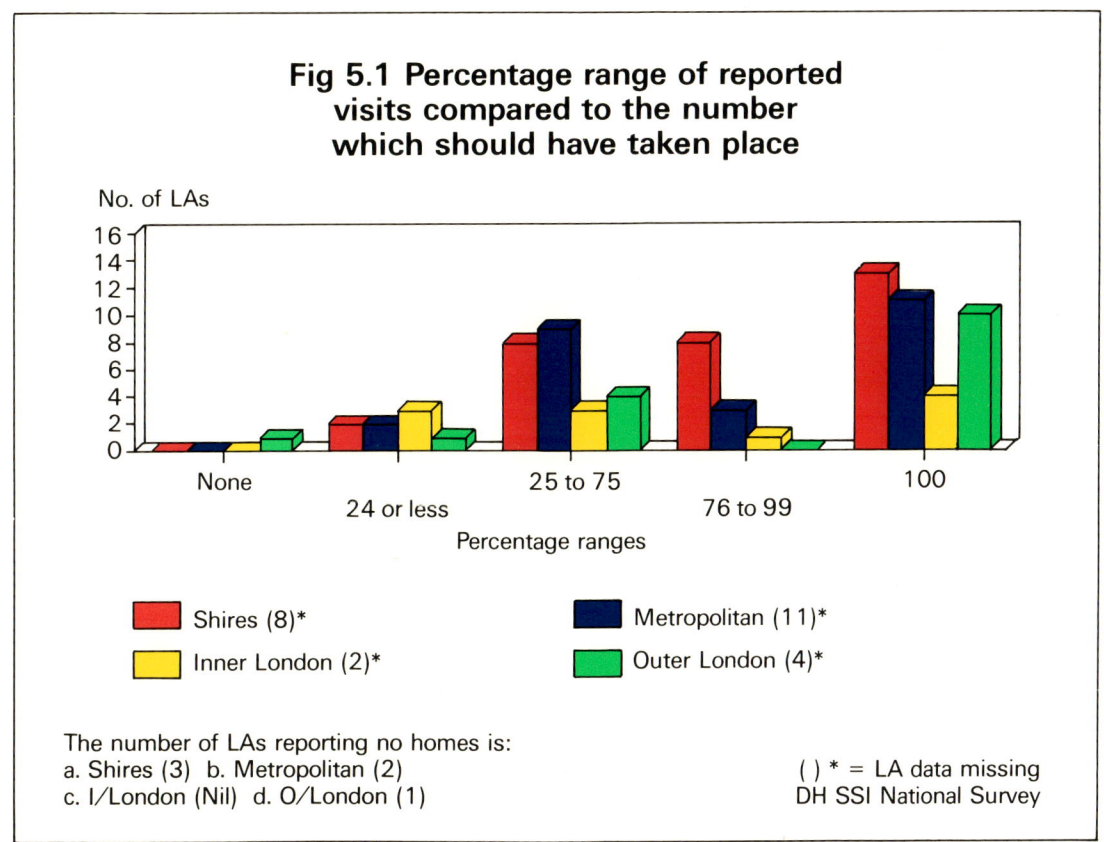

Fig 5.1 Percentage range of reported visits compared to the number which should have taken place

No. of LAs

Percentage ranges

None 24 or less 25 to 75 76 to 99 100

Shires (8)* Metropolitan (11)*
Inner London (2)* Outer London (4)*

The number of LAs reporting no homes is:
a. Shires (3) b. Metropolitan (2)
c. I/London (Nil) d. O/London (1)

( ) * = LA data missing
DH SSI National Survey

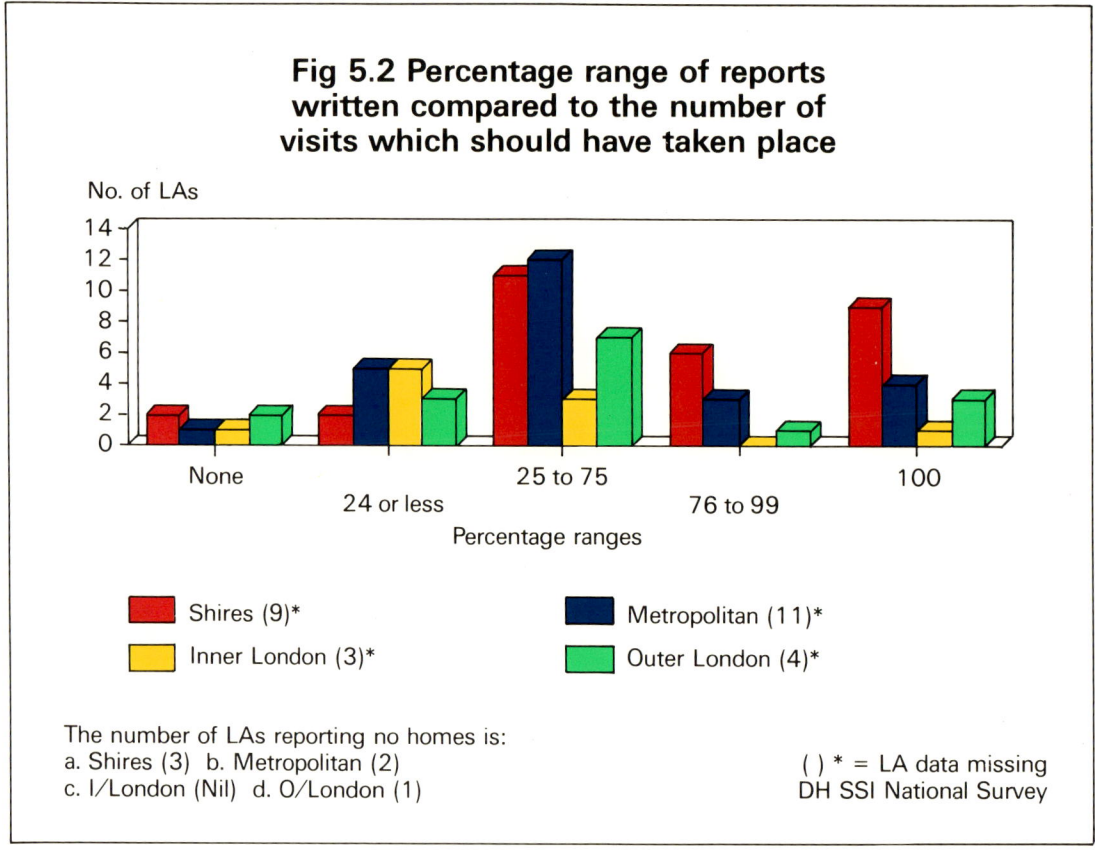

Fig 5.2 Percentage range of reports written compared to the number of visits which should have taken place

Legend:
- Shires (9)*
- Metropolitan (11)*
- Inner London (3)*
- Outer London (4)*

The number of LAs reporting no homes is:
a. Shires (3) b. Metropolitan (2)
c. I/London (Nil) d. O/London (1)

( ) * = LA data missing
DH SSI National Survey

5.29   These figures suggest that authorities are finding this an onerous responsibility which many are failing to meet in full. The Department attaches great importance to this duty as a significant contribution to safeguarding the welfare of children in residential care. The Local Authority Associations, in pursuit of a recommendation in the Utting report, are writing guidance to help elected members meet these responsibilities and these disappointing indications will be brought to their attention.

Registration of Private Children's Homes

5.30   The effect of section 63(3) of the Children Act 1989 was to replace the Children's Homes Act 1982 (which was never brought into force). Since 14 October 1991 private homes which provide for more than three children must be registered with the local authority.

5.31   The survey revealed that by the end of June 1992 170 applications for registration of private homes had been received by local authorities. In each case the registration authority is required to cause the home to be inspected before deciding whether or not to grant the application.

5.32   Of the 170 applications received 221 inspections are reported to have taken place. This could be explained by the fact that two visits a year are required. However it is also possible that authorities have entered the number of visits rather than the number of inspections.

5.33   By June only 20 private children's homes were reported to have been registered; one home had been refused registration. The Department reminded authorities in August 1992 of the provision in the Children Act whereby an application for registration as a registered children's home which has not been granted or refused within twelve months of being lodged with the local authority is to be deemed to have been refused. This slow progress towards completing registration following receipt of applications is therefore a matter of considerable concern.

Registration of Section 63 Schools—Independent schools with 50 or fewer boarders required to register as registered (ie private) children's homes

5.34   The programme of preparatory work for inspections of independent schools generally, described in the next chapter, did not directly address the requirements to be met by schools required to register under Section 63. However such schools share many common features with those with larger numbers of boarders and authorities were advised to take a similarly flexible approach to their work with them. Even so, it is clear that more difficulties have been experienced in the case of schools required to register as children's homes than for those subject to S87 of the Act. Experience quickly showed that some requirements of the regulations are difficult to apply in the case of some schools. This has led to some reluctance to progress the new provisions as quickly as might have been expected and to a number of complaints to Ministers.

5.35   Many schools and SSDs found particular difficulty in determining how to apply the detailed requirements of the Children's Homes Regulations 1991 to the daily operation of organisations which saw themselves primarily as schools rather than homes. Indeed, there is some evidence that there has been considerable resistance to this requirement for schools to register and some schools are believed to be holding out against registering in the hope that the Children Act might be amended to redefine schools required to register as homes. However although such a change in the law is under active consideration, this would take some time before it could come into force. In the meantime, in response to growing belief that some easement in the burden of the regulations should be given to at least some of the schools, the Department consulted with other agencies about possible changes to the regulations in the Spring of 1992. The responses to the consultation, and possible changes in regulations which would ease their impact on schools where the majority of the children return to their families at holiday times, are now being considered.

5.36   The survey showed that 140 applications from schools had been received by local authorities. It is known from the Department for Education that there are approximately 250 schools required to register as children's homes and local authorities were provided in 1991 with the names and addresses of the schools concerned. The Children Act requires schools subject to S63 to initiate application for registration but, unless they have already done so the Department of Health would expect that social services departments should initiate contacts with all relevant schools urgently.

5.37   Again the number of inspections—148—is reported as exceeding the number of applications but the same possible explanations apply as for private homes which are not schools. Only 19 of these 140 applications are reported to have been registered. None have been refused registration. Local authority responses to these applications for homes and schools seem to vary enormously, with some local authorities appearing to have done no inspections and others having done far more inspections than there are homes and schools—up to 7 inspections per home (not schools) in one case.

Wales

5.38   There are 62 local authority children's homes in Wales as well as 4 voluntary homes and 6 private children's homes. These provide places for about 650 children. A total of 13 establishments have made applications to local authorities in Wales to register under section 63. Five of these applications have come from independent schools. The registration process has been completed for one home. The applications for the remaining twelve as of October 1992 were still under consideration.

Voluntary Children's Homes

5.39   Prior to the Children Act 1989, voluntary children's homes were required to be registered by the Secretary of State. The Regulations governing the conduct of the homes dated from 1951. These homes were and continue to be inspected by the Social Services Inspectorate under powers provided by the Secretary of State.

5.40   This registration procedure remains unaltered by the 1989 Act. Voluntary children's homes are, however, now subject to the Children's Homes Regulations 1991 which also govern the conduct of private homes and local authority community homes for children.

Chapter 6: Independent Schools

Background

6.1   Under Section 87 of the Children Act those responsible for independent schools are required to safeguard and promote the welfare of boarders and local authorities have a duty to satisfy themselves that this requirement is being met. As a result the welfare arrangements of around 750 independent boarding schools come within the purview of social services for the first time. Well over 100,000 children are affected by the changes.

6.2   The need to make additional provision regarding boarding schools was recognised during the passage of the Children Act as a result of events at Crookham Court, a privately owned school. It was found that boys at the school were sexually abused over a number of years by the proprietor and staff. Cases of similar abuse at other schools have confirmed the need to ensure that children in them are protected.

6.3   Guidance was issued jointly by the Department of Health and the Department for Education to local authority social services departments and independent boarding schools in 1991 in Volume 5 in the Children Act Guidance and Regulations series. The Guidance advised social services and schools of their duties under Section 87. Volume 5 also included guidance on the standards expected to be applied by social services departments in carrying out their duties under Section 87. This was for the benefit of both social services and the schools, so that the former would be clear about those matters that were their proper concern under Section 87 and the latter would know what would be expected of them. The Secretary of State for Education would not be expected to take action against a school on the basis of a report by social services under Section 87 unless social services had stated the grounds on which they had formed the view that a school had failed to safeguard the welfare of the child; these grounds would have to be able to be sustained by reference to the guidance on standards in Volume 5.

6.4   Volume 5 gives advice on management, child protection procedures, staffing, accommodation, health, safety, contacts with parents and others, religious and cultural ethos, discipline, restriction of liberty, and complaints procedures.

6.5   In addition the Inspection of Premises, Children and Records (Independent Schools) Regulations 1991 gave powers to social services departments to inspect the schools to enable them to carry out their duties.

Implementation Programme

6.6   These new provisions presented a considerable challenge both to social services, needing to develop skills in a new field, and to the schools becoming subject to this kind of scrutiny for the first time. Consequently an extensive programme of preparatory work was undertaken by SSI, HMI, the Department of Health and Department of Education and Science (as it then was). Twelve pilot inspections were mounted, carried out by social services departments and representatives of the schools, with support from SSI and HMI. Based on this work seminars were arranged in each region, bringing school and social services representatives together to consider the implications of the new duties.

6.7   The lessons of the programme were disseminated in a Practice Guide and Training Pack. "The Children Act 1989, The Welfare of Children in Boarding Schools, Practice Guide, Department of Health, Social Services Inspectorate, HMSO", was published in 1991 and circulated to all social services departments and boarding schools. The Training Pack "Independent Schools with Boarding—An Induction Programme for Social Services Inspectors, Trainers and Managers", Department of Health, Social Services Inspectorate, HMSO, was published in 1992 and also widely circulated.

6.8   The need for sound preparatory work was one of the key messages deriving from the pilot inspections. Personal contacts to establish communication, brief initial visits to schools to assess the scale of the inspection task and establishing mechanisms for agreement about methods and standards were also emphasised. Some of this work began in the programme of regional seminars and many social services departments established their own preparatory and consultative programmes at an early stage. It is also apparent that some schools were making equally careful preparation, for instance by reviewing school procedures and staff training and in making specific changes such as the provision of telephones for pupils' use or improving the privacy of bathing arrangements. In these cases, the introduction of the new systems appears to have been achieved smoothly with relatively few problems despite the very considerable scale of the task involved.

Inspections

6.9　　The national monitoring survey showed that there were 731 schools governed by Section 87 known to the 68 local authorities which responded.

6.10　　Of these schools 254 (or 35%) had been inspected (Guidance suggests an inspection of each school within a year from 14 October 1992) . The survey shows a small number of local authorities with significant numbers of schools which appear to have made no efforts to tackle Section 87 inspections.

6.11　　These figures may be misleading. Anecdotal evidence available to the Social Services Inspectorate indicates that in many areas there had been very active communication between SSDs and schools and it may be therefore that the number of schools "visited" as opposed to "inspected" may be higher than shown by the survey.

6.12　　The wide variation in the distribution of schools between authorities is apparent from the survey:

Schools	Authorities
No schools known	40
Between 1 and 9	39
Between 10 and 19	13
Between 20 and 29	8
30 and upwards	8

What the survey does not show however are the equally dramatic variations in the size of the schools, which may have between 1 and 25 boarding houses and provide for between 50 and 1,000 pupils in total. There is therefore a very wide variation in the workload falling on individual authorities.

6.13　　A concern about the rate of progress relates to the variation between authorities (see figure 6.1). Some 11 authorities (10% of the total) report completing 100% of the required inspections (although only two of these authorities had more than 2 schools to inspect). At the other end of the scale it is of most concern that 31 authorities, over one-third of the total, had not completed any inspections and this group included some authorities responsible for inspecting very large numbers of schools. In between 7 authorities had completed 50% or more of their target including some authorities with large programmes to complete. A further 19 authorities had done some inspections amounting to less than 50% of their target.

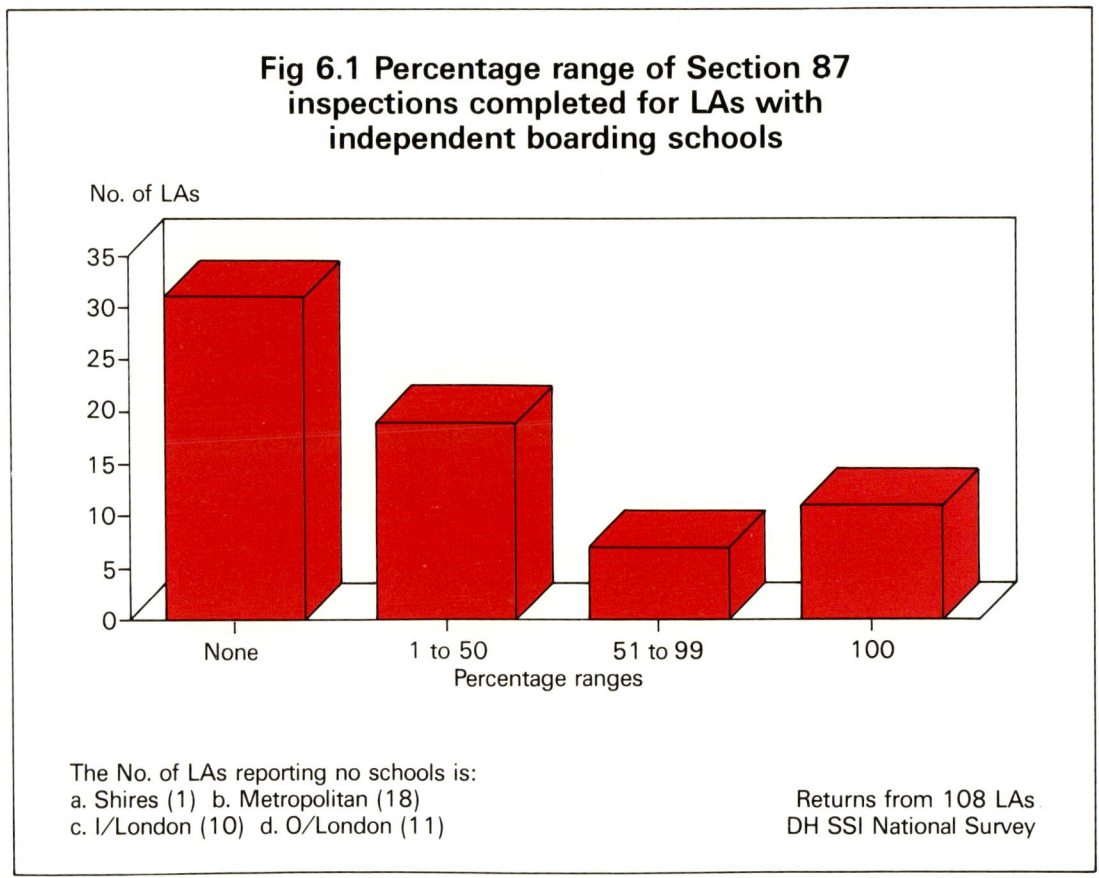

Fig 6.1 Percentage range of Section 87 inspections completed for LAs with independent boarding schools

No. of LAs

Percentage ranges

None   1 to 50   51 to 99   100

The No. of LAs reporting no schools is:
a. Shires (1) b. Metropolitan (18)
c. I/London (10) d. O/London (11)

Returns from 108 LAs
DH SSI National Survey

6.14   While there is a measure of flexibility in the guidance the evidence suggests that a significant number of authorities, particularly those reporting completion of no or very few inspections need to review their position and ensure that initial visits are undertaken as soon as possible.

6.15   The size of the school, the number of boarding houses to be inspected, or the complexity of the task, may mean that the initial visit does not amount to a full inspection. Authorities however need to be able to demonstrate that at least an initial assessment has been made of all the schools they are responsible for to deal with immediate concerns and as the basis of priority setting for further contacts.

6.16   The Children Act requires that where a local authority social services department forms the view that there has been a failure by those responsible for an independent boarding school to comply with their welfare duty under Section 87 of the Act the local authority has a duty to notify the Secretary of State (for Education) who in turn can consider action under the Education Act 1944 which could (ultimately) lead to the closure of this school. No such notifications have been made to date (but see paragraph 6.18).

6.17   In addition to the duty to give formal notice when the Social Services department is of the opinion that there has been a failure in the welfare duty, advice was given in guidance that copies of all inspection reports should be provided to the Department for Education. It is important that the registration authority has an up-to-date picture of the views of the social services department responsible for assessing the welfare of pupils at a school, whether or not there has been any failure on the part of the school. Information available from the Department for Education indicates that the number of reports received amounts to only 115. This is well below the number of inspections reported in the survey to have been completed. Advice on the form of reports and notification was also given in The Welfare of Children in Boarding Schools Practice Guide at Chapter 7. Of these 115 reports, Department for Education advise that some 10% of reports registered criticisms which have required follow-up action by HMI. Examples of the deficiencies noted relate predominantly to standards of accommodation resulting in some instances in a lack of privacy particularly for older children.

6.18 Cases have been identified where it has been necessary to examine whether children have been harmed by members of staff or other pupils and this information has been conveyed to the Department of Health and the Department for Education. Some of these cases have required investigation under local Child Protection Procedures including by the Police and have led to action being taken against alleged abusers. Other instances have been reported to the Departments or to Ministers where a school and social services department have been unable to agree on methods or standards to be applied. Some arose because of the unwillingness of the school to accept the new inspection arrangements, others because the inspection proposed by the responsible social services was unnecessarily intrusive. Particular difficulties have related to the extent of private contacts which some inspectors have sought to have with pupils, particularly the youngest ones, or to the widespread use of detailed questionnaires for completion by pupils.

6.19 A number of areas where there is difficulty in determining best practice are also emerging, for example in cases where lodgings are used to provide term-time accommodation for pupils or where schools need to make arrangements for pupils during short holidays because they are unable to return to homes in distant countries. Such cases emphasise the need for continuing dialogue about development of this new area of practice. A number of social services departments have arranged meetings to review the first year's operation of the new procedures in their own area involving the schools concerned. These are valuable initiatives and worth considering in other areas also. A national seminar is to be held by SSI in May 1993 in association with the National Children's Bureau. This will provide an opportunity for schools and social services to review practice issues and identify specific problems and achievements. Consideration will be given to mounting a second similar seminar if demand proves to be sufficiently high.

Chapter 7: Leaving Care

Background

7.1   The successful re-integration of young people with their families or other responsible people or, where this is not possible or practicable, enabling young people to move successfully to independence, are objectives for all children being looked after by local authorities. The Children Act recognises the vital importance of preparing children properly for this step by placing a duty on authorities to advise, assist and befriend every child they are looking after with a view to promoting their welfare when they cease to be looked after. For simplicity, the terms 'leaving care' will be used to describe the process of 'ceasing to be looked after' and 'aftercare' the provision of support to those who are no longer 'looked after'.

7.2   Under the terms of Part III of the Act children leaving care after reaching the age of 16 can look to the authority for continued aftercare support until they reach the age of 21. Aftercare support may be provided by local authorities through offering advice and befriending to those who seek their help and by offering assistance in kind or, exceptionally, in cash. Similarly, children leaving a variety of voluntary and private placements or accommodation provided by health and education authorities, may also seek the aftercare support of local authorities. Authorities have additional powers to assist children they had been looking after by contributing to accommodation expenses incurred in connection with employment, education or training, and to provide grants for educational or training purposes.

7.3   The legal framework which enables local authorities to provide such aftercare support is not prescriptive but is provided in general terms. This flexibility recognises the diversity of children leaving care and enables authorities to tailor aftercare support to the needs of the individual child. The general expectation is that local authorities should act as any responsible parent in offering support and assistance.

7.4   As with other Part III functions, the Act enables local authorities to seek the help of other authorities or persons to help them carry out their aftercare responsibilities. Where such help is sought, authorities are required to comply with the request provided it is compatible with their own statutory responsibilities and does not prejudice the discharge of any of their functions. Such inter-agency co-operation is a key factor in the development of an effective aftercare service.

7.5   Local authorities are required to publish information about 'leaving care' and 'aftercare' services and to take such steps as are practicable to ensure that such information is drawn to the attention of those who might benefit from them. Authorities have been advised that, in preparing such information, they will need to take account of the differing needs of young people according to their age, sex and maturity. The special needs of certain groups of young people (e.g. those with disabilities or special educational needs, pregnant girls or those with babies, or from a range of cultural, racial and linguistic backgrounds) also need to be taken into account.

Preparation for Leaving Care

7.6   The statutory requirement on local authorities to prepare all children they are looking after for the time when they leave care was a new duty, although it did no more than reinforce what had already been good practice in many settings (an identical requirement was placed on voluntary organisations accommodating children and those providing registered children's homes in the private sector). As far as local authorities are concerned, it is important to note that the duty to 'prepare' applies to every child they look after, irrespective of age or length of placement. In other words, the duty does not just apply to those who will be leaving care after reaching the age of 16 years. This underlines the importance of developing a clear 'preparation' policy which reflects the wide variety of circumstances in which children can be looked after.

7.7 The following information about local authority provision for young people leaving care was collected in a separate survey undertaken by First Key, the National Leaving Care Advisory Service, in the Summer of 1992[1]. The survey results mirror the outcome of similar studies undertaken in mid-1992 by the media and other voluntary organisations.

7.8 Only some 50% of local authorities had developed formal written policies on preparation for leaving care. A further 19% had such work in hand (see figure 7.1). Given the emphasis placed in the Department's Guidance on the importance of good quality preparation, the fact that staff in half the authorities in the country did not have a clear framework within which to develop consistent and effective preparation programmes is a cause for concern.

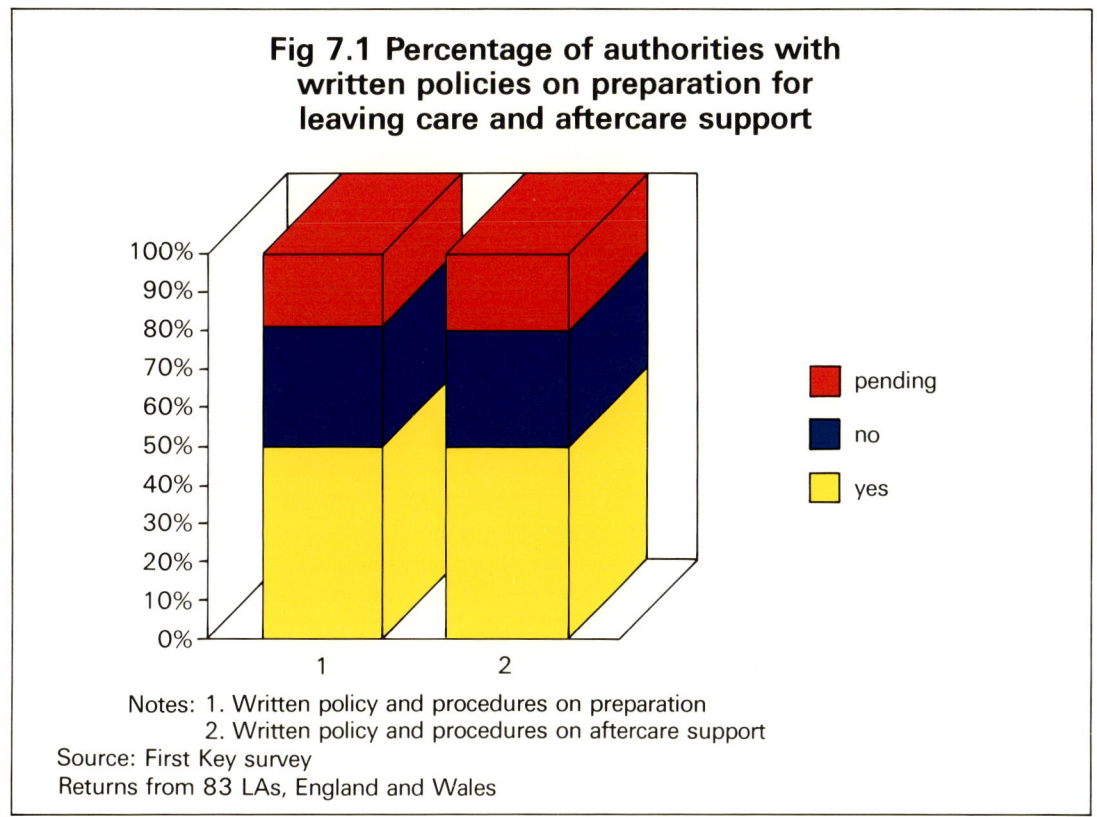

Fig 7.1 Percentage of authorities with written policies on preparation for leaving care and aftercare support

Notes: 1. Written policy and procedures on preparation
2. Written policy and procedures on aftercare support
Source: First Key survey
Returns from 83 LAs, England and Wales

7.9 As noted above, however, good practice in the 'preparation' of children for leaving care could be found in a wide variety of settings prior to implementation of the Act. For example, many individual community homes had built this into their day to day programmes. Some have independence units where children approaching the time when they leave care can be helped to develop the social and practical skills needed to move to independence. Similarly, individual foster parents had seen this as part of their ongoing responsibilities when caring for children on behalf of the authority. Examples of good practice can be found even in those authorities which do not currently have a formal written policy. The challenge for the future will be to ensure that comprehensive policies are developed and implemented in every authority which reflect the diversity of each child's needs, whether their care plan is for a return home or to independent living.

After Care Support

7.10 A similar picture can be found in the development of formal written policies for the provision of aftercare support. About half the authorities have completed this task while a further 20% have such work in hand (see figure 7.1 above). Some two-thirds of the authorities have drawn up written agreements with other agencies covering cooperation in the delivery of services (for example, over the provision of accommodation).

---

[1] First Key/DH commissioned survey of local authority provision for young people leaving care was published 30 November 1992. Responses were received (at the time of compiling the Report) from 88 or 76% of the 116 authorities in England and Wales.

7.11 Again, there had been a wide variation between authorities in the development of aftercare support prior to implementation of the Act. Some had specialist officers in post. In others, aftercare support was provided by the child's social worker or by residential care staff in the home where the child had last been accommodated. In many areas foster parents played an important role in providing advice and support for those they had previously looked after, or by continuing to provide accommodation on an informal basis. These arrangements have continued since implementation of the Act and provide the foundations on which further developments can be built.

Publicity of Services

7.12 In addition to the development of formal written policies to guide the direction of the local delivery of services, it is important that these services should be publicised so that staff know what is expected of them and children and their parents are aware of the help which can be made available. In addition, an explicit statement of intent provides the yardstick against which representations about the discharge by the authority of its preparation and aftercare functions can be judged. The Department has recommended that guides outlining the aftercare services the local authority can provide should be produced for children leaving care. It is disappointing to record that only one-fifth of authorities have so far produced specific guidance for children, while a further one-third have such guidance in hand.[2]

Leaving Care Grants

7.13 To date information is not available about the number of children who, having left care, have sought the support of the local authority. From surveys undertaken during the previous twelve months, and recently published research, however, it is clear that jobs, housing and levels of financial support are the major topics of concern to care leavers. Nearly all local authorities provide care leavers with a leaving care grant. The prime purpose of such grants is to assist young people to meet the necessary costs of setting up home, or entering employment or further education. The level of such support, however, varies widely between and within individual authorities (see figure 7.2). Maximum payments awarded range from £63 to £2,000 for individual children, with a national average of a maximum of £731. Many young people would, of course, receive far less than these figures or receive no grant at all.

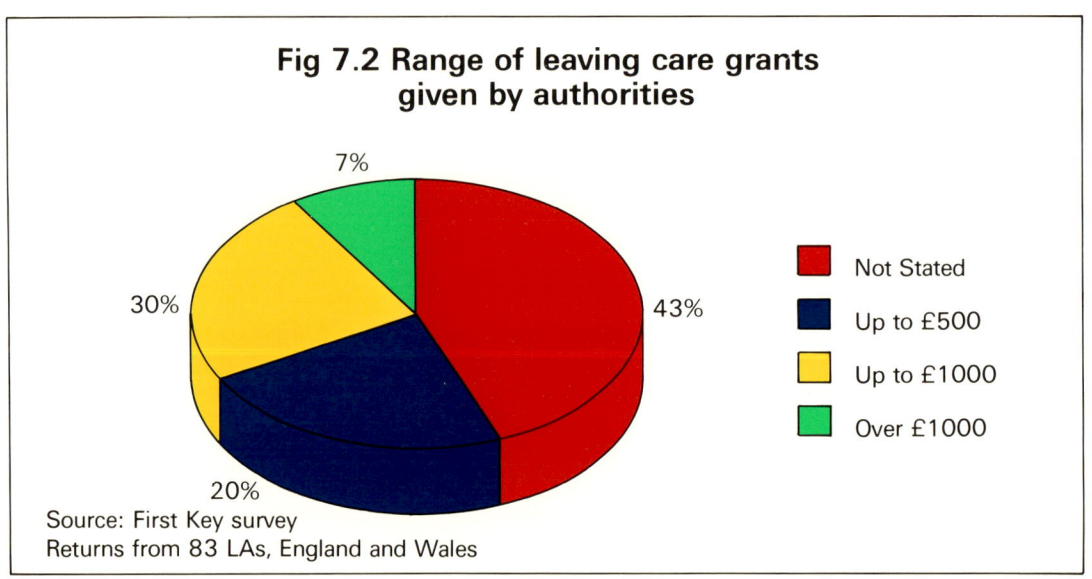

Fig 7.2 Range of leaving care grants given by authorities

7%
30%
43%
20%

Not Stated
Up to £500
Up to £1000
Over £1000

Source: First Key survey
Returns from 83 LAs, England and Wales

---

[2] These figures are lower than those revealed by the national monitoring survey (table 3.9). This may be explained by the fact that some local authorities who responded to the First Key survey that they have not produced their own guides are, nonetheless using guides prepared by other agencies.

Research, Training and Consultancy

7.14   In order to assist local authorities to improve the quality of preparation and aftercare service delivery the Department of Health has taken a number of steps:

- the University of Leeds has been commissioned to undertake research to evaluate the effectiveness of various forms of aftercare service delivery;

- the preparation of training materials has been commissioned for staff working in social services departments and the voluntary sector on the aftercare provisions of the Act;

- 'First Key,' the National Leaving Care Advisory Service, continues to be supported to provide advice and consultancy to local authorities to assist in the development of good preparation and aftercare practice.

7.15   In Wales a 3 year grant aided project has been sponsored to review developments in all 8 authorities and to conduct an in depth study of policy and practice in one urban and one rural authority. The first stage of the project, being undertaken by Swansea University is almost finished.

General

7.16   While much progress has been made in responding to the new preparation and aftercare provisions of the Act, it is clear that the overall picture remains fragmented and patchy. The fact that a substantial proportion of authorities have still to formally address the expanded aftercare responsibilities placed on them by the Act is a cause for concern. It is also disappointing that, a year after implementation, so few authorities have so far published information about the range of aftercare services they can make available. Without clear statements of policy or service provision, staff have no agreed framework within which a consistent service to young people who seek their help and support can be provided. Similarly, young people themselves are disadvantaged in not knowing to what services they can reasonably expect to have access. The failures of management to address these issues will need to be a focus of attention in the coming year.

7.17   Against that, it is important to acknowledge the positive way in which many practitioners are working with individual care leavers and the effective partnerships which are being developed within many authorities with the voluntary and private sectors. It will be important over the coming year to ensure that information about best practice is more widely disseminated.

Chapter 8: The Guardian *ad litem*and Reporting Officer Service

Background

8.1 Guardians *ad litem*are appointed by the courts in specified family proceedings. Their role is to represent the child before the court on what is in his or her best interests and to ensure that the child's wishes and feelings are made clear to the court. The paramountcy of the welfare of the child and the requirement that the voice of the child should be heard when decisions are being made about his or her future are, of course, central principles of the Act. The guardian therefore, has a crucial role to play in helping to ensure that in the courts the Act works as Parliament intended and that the principles of the Act are reflected in practice.

Panel Membership

8.2 Guardians are usually qualified social workers with considerable experience of child care matters and a sound understanding of family law. Guardians on panels are drawn from the following categories:

- self employed social workers (full-time or part-time);

- employees of a local authority (full-time or part-time);

- employees of a voluntary organisation (full-time or part-time);

- probation officers.

Those persons who are employed part-time as probation officers may, in the remainder of their time, act as panel members in respect of care and adoption proceedings, whereas if they are panel members as serving probation officers their role is restricted to adoption proceedings.

8.3 It is essential that guardians are able to bring completely independent professional judgement to a case. To ensure this, there are four categories of persons who, although they may be appointed as members of the panel, must not be appointed for specified proceedings in particular cases. Subject to certain exceptions, persons excluded from appointment to certain cases include any panel member who is:

- a member, officer or servant of a local authority where that local authority is a party to the proceedings (unless employed solely as a panel member);

- a member, officer or servant of the NSPCC where that organisation is bringing care or other proceedings under the Act;

- a serving probation officer;

- a member, officer or servant of a local authority or voluntary organisation who are involved or who have been involved, with that child.

8.4 Whether panel members are employed solely by local authorities as panel members full-time or part-time, or are employed by voluntary organisations, the intention is to ensure that a guardian is not appointed to a case if formerly that person "has been directly concerned in that capacity in arrangements relating to the care, accommodation or welfare of the child during the five years prior to the commencement of the proceedings".

8.5 The Department has not recommended recruitment from any one source rather than another. It is left to be determined by local authorities having regard to the needs of their area. The composition of panels varies widely round the country. Some panels are wholly composed of self employed members, some of employed guardians and in others a mixture of the two. The contribution made by the Probation Service varies from one area to another. The figures in Table 8.1 suggest that Panel membership has moved towards a more concentrated, dedicated workforce in line with the Social Services Inspectorate recommendations. Moreover there has been a significant increase in the proportion of fee attracting self employed guardians (more than 50% at 31 March 1992) at the expense of local authority employed guardians.

TABLE 8.1　Panel Membership 31 March 1992*

(Figures based on returns from 55 out of 56 Panels)

Voluntary Organisations	Probation	Local Authority Employees	Fee-attracting Self Employed	Total
56	146	373	752	1,327
4.2%	11%	28.1%	56.6%	

Panel Membership 1989/90*

(Figures based on those obtained for the 1990 Social Services Inspectorate report and drawn from 56 out of 61 Panels)

Voluntary Organisations	Probation	Local Authority Employees	Fee-attracting Self Employed	Total
87	392	1,189	668	2,366[1]
3.7%	16.6%	50.3%	28.2%	

*　These figures are persons in membership not full time equivalent. Fee attracting guardians in membership of more than one panel will have been counted more than once.

[1]　Total includes 30 "Others" not identified.

Functions of a GALRO

8.6　Guardians *ad litem* and reporting officers are not a new creation of the Children Act. They have been in existence since 1984 with the full implementation of the 1975 Children Act guardian service. The 1989 Act, however, gives guardians an enhanced role in family proceedings. There is both a presumption in favour of appointing guardians in a wider range of proceedings and at an earlier stage and they are required to adopt a more pro-active stance and have been given a wider range of duties.

8.7　The specified proceedings set out in the Act include all care and related public proceedings and emergency protection order proceedings. By Rules of Court these have now been extended to include secure accommodation applications, applications to extend a supervision order, applications by a local authority to change a child's surname or arrange for a child subject to a care order to live outside England and Wales; and appeals in any such proceedings. Working with the court the guardian *ad litem* will seek to ensure that the proceedings are conducted effectively and completed in the shortest possible timespan.

8.8　The task of the guardian as prescribed in the Rules of Court demands a considerable analytical capability and well developed inter personal skills. The situation in which he or she is involved is inevitably fraught with difficulties. The guardian is called upon to make careful assessments of complex family relationships and based on these to predict what is likely to be the best future option for a child. There is frequently considerable conflict and immense stress within the family with whom the guardian is working. There may also be substantial differences in perception between the various professionals concerned with the child and the guardian as to where the best long term interests of the child lie.

Managed Service

8.9　The enhanced role of the guardian under the Act made it even more important than before that an efficient high quality service should be available to the courts. Prior to the Act coming into force, the Department of Health recognised the legitimate concerns that existed in some parts of the country about the availability of guardians. The inspection of the service carried out by the Social Services Inspectorate in 1990 had highlighted the need for a more managed service. The Department responded to these findings when drawing up the new arrangements for the service under the Act. The emphasis on effective management was signalled clearly in the Panel Regulations and in the accompanying guidance.

8.10 Responsibility for the provision of the service remains with the local authority as was the case before October 1991. Local authorities' duties in respect of the guardian service are set out clearly and more specifically than before in the Guardians *ad litem* and Reporting Officers (Panels) Regulations.

8.11 Since October 1991 great progress has been made in all panels towards achieving a managed service. Panel managers are in post; sufficient guardians have been appointed; effective administrative procedures are being introduced in respect of appointment and re-appointment to the panel, monitoring of the work of panel members and the handling of complaints. Panels are undertaking reviews of their systems for ensuring prompt appointment of guardians to individual cases. An increasing number of panels are acquiring computerised management information systems which will enable them to exercise more effective control over the work of the panel. Panel committees are in place and playing a valuable role sharing the management functions with the panel manager. Guardians themselves through their membership of the panel committees are playing a more active role in the management of the service.

8.12 There is a diversity of arrangements throughout the country for the delivery of the service. These existed before the implementation of the Children Act and had developed to take account of local circumstances. Arrangements include reciprocal arrangements between two neighbouring authorities, groups of authorities linked with varying degrees of formality in consortia, single local authority panels and contracts placed with voluntary organisations to provide the service. The Department in its guidance did not advocate any one arrangement in preference to any other but advised a careful assessment locally of the varying merits of the possible options. At the time of writing the report the position is as set out below.

> Number of GALRO Panels—56
> Number of Joint Consortium Panels—12
> Number of Single Authority Panels—44
> Number of panels where the service has been contracted out wholly or partly to voluntary organisations—6

Independence of the Service

8.13 The freedom to choose whatever arrangements best suit the local circumstances is not, however, absolute. The service has to be provided in accordance with the Panels Regulations and accompanying guidance together with the Rules of Court. The right of a child to separate and independent representation in public law proceedings is a central principle of the Act. There clearly could be potential for conflict where the authority responsible for the provision of the guardian service is a party to proceedings in which a guardian has been appointed to act for the child. This was recognised and a range of safeguards was built into the regulations, guidance and Rules of Court to underpin the independence of the guardian in the exercise of his or her professional judgement. These include the appointment of a panel manager who is independent of the child care services management, establishment of a panel committee with independent representation and the setting up of a complaints procedure again with an independent element.

8.14 Nonetheless concerns continue to be expressed about the independence of the service despite the existence of these safeguards. Clearly if there is any suggestion that a guardian in reaching his or her professional judgement as to what is in the best interests of the child is not able for any reason to exercise independence then this is a matter to be brought to the attention of the court. Since the Act came into force, however, there is little by way of documented evidence of efforts by local authorities to constrain the independence of the guardian. One noted instance occurred prior to the implementation of the Act. It arose from the imposition by a local authority of a prescriptive limit on the time a guardian could spend on any one case. An application for Judicial Review was brought and was upheld.[2] The President of the Family Division, Sir Stephen Brown, found that the Director of Social Services in imposing the time limit had exceeded the proper

---

[2] R v Cornwall County Council (1992) 1 WLR 427.

exercise of his authority which in that case amounted to an abuse of power. The decision to impose a benchmark scheme sought to restrict the discretion of the guardian to undertake work the guardian might consider necessary. Further, the Director had imposed this in an arbitrary manner. The President commended the 1991 guidance which was in force by the time the judgment was given. It emphasises the importance of a partnership approach between panel managers and panel members in determining what is a reasonable time to spend on individual cases. On anecdotal evidence the management in partnership approach appears to be working well round the country.

GALROs in Private Law Proceedings

8.15   Some confusion has been encountered as to the role of a panel guardian when invited to act in private law proceedings. Under the Children Act the court will appoint a panel guardian (ie appointed to a panel established in accordance with Regulations) for the child in specified public law proceedings, unless satisfied that it is not necessary to do so. There is no provision under the Act to appoint panel guardians in private law proceedings. The usual approach, endorsed by the Court of Appeal[3] is that a divorce court welfare officer's report should suffice. In exceptional circumstances, and only in the High Court and County Courts the Official Solicitor may be invited to act. The Lord Chancellor's Department has issued guidance as to the kind of cases which that office will be prepared to consider. If the Official Solicitor intervenes he may "contract" this work to guardians some of whom may be panel guardians—to act as his agents. In these cases the guardian's reasonable costs will be met by the Official Solicitor.

Training

8.16   The enhanced role of the guardian and the extended role of the panel manager made it necessary to provide practice guidance to assist both managers and guardians to carry out their tasks effectively. Accordingly the Department commissioned separate handbooks for guardians and for panel managers, as part of the Training Support Programme. These were published in the summer of 1992 and distributed widely to panel members and to managers with copies made available to social services departments, panel committees and members of complaints boards. A further guide for guardians will be available in the Spring. It builds on the first handbook but concerns itself especially with court craft.

8.17   Many guardians participated generally in the comprehensive training programme leading up to implementation of the Children Act but additional training courses aimed specifically at guardians were run by the National Association of Guardians ad litem and Reporting Officers (NAGALRO). The Department was able to provide some funding towards these and Departmental Officials led some of the sessions in the seminars on the role of the guardian in secure accommodation applications. The Department has since made further monies available for courses organised by the National Association. These will be used for both induction courses for guardians and also courses targeted at specific areas of expertise relevant to guardian duties. In addition, before and since October 1991 the Department has funded consultants to work with panels round the country in improving their administrative systems to cope with the challenges the Act presents.

Financial Support: The Specific Grant

8.18   In addition to the support for training guardians ad litem, the Department has demonstrated its commitment to an effective guardian service by the decision to fund the further responsibilities placed upon the service by the Act by means of a specific grant—that is ring fenced money which is to be used exclusively for the guardian service. The grant totalling £5.7 million for 1992/93 has been distributed amongst authorities using a formula based on two factors (i) the population aged under 18 in the local authority area (ii) the number of children admitted to local authority care during the year averaged over the three years 1988-90. Twenty per cent of the overall grant was held in reserve for allocation where authorities found themselves under financial pressures in respect of the guardian service. The eligibility criteria for payment of the grant were:—

> (i) that a panel manager, appropriately located within the organisation and with appropriate responsibilities had to be in post;
>
> (ii) the panel committee and complaints board had to be established.

---

[3]   Re H (Minors) unreported.

8.19 The powers to introduce a specific grant in support of GALRO panel services have not been invoked in Wales. Grant support is available to local authorities under the "Support for Child and Family Services" grant scheme (operated under Section 28B(1)(a) of the National Health Service Act, 1977 as amended). A consortium of 3 authorities (Gwent, Mid Glamorgan and Powys) made an application for grant for 1992/93 to support 75% of the costs of the administration of a cooperative Guardian *ad litem*panel. They were offered a grant of £48,420. No bids were made by other authorities in Wales.

Quality of Service

8.20 Before October 1991 a shortage of guardians in some parts of the country resulted in considerable delays in guardians starting work on cases. It is generally agreed that delay is likely to affect adversely the wellbeing of the child and the avoidance of unnecessary delay is one of the central principles of the Act. The data supplied by local authorities in connection with their bid for the specific grant and the information contained in the annual reports indicate that there are now sufficient guardians to undertake work promptly and within the time scales set by the court.

8.21 It is more difficult to make an objective assessment of the quality of the work being undertaken by the guardians in their investigations and reports and the assistance they give to the courts. There are no nationally agreed reliable measures of this. The Department will be undertaking more work on developing agreed standards which would be the hallmark of a high quality service. Further studies will also help to identify which models of service are best able to deliver a combination of high quality provision for the child together with value for money.

8.22 The Department, sought to build in measures to promote quality into its guidance on panel management. The guidance requires that guardians should in most cases be qualified social workers with several years of relevant experience working with children and with an aptitude for the demands and disciplines of the type of work. Guardians are required to be subject to rigorous selection procedures prior to appointment and regular reviews subsequently. Reappointment is by no means automatic.

8.23 The National Association of Guardians *ad litem*and Reporting Officers to which most guardians belong has an explicit code of ethics to which its members are required to adhere. This helps to set high standards for the profession.

Monitoring the Service

8.24 Two main sources of written information are available at present. These are data supplied by local authorities in connection with their claims for the specific grant and that contained in the annual reports. Information collated from the specific grant returns forwarded by each local authority reveals a total expenditure on the guardian service in the period 1 April 1992–30 September 1992 of almost £6.2 million or approximately £12.4 million for the year assuming a similar rate of appointment of guardians and expenditure on the service as a whole.

8.25 In the period 1 April 1992 to 30 September 1992 there were 7,546 individual applications in public law proceedings in which a guardian was appointed. This suggests an annual total in excess of 15,000 if the same level of appointment continued throughout the year. Approximately 42 per cent of these appointments are in relation to adoption applications.

8.26 The guidance accompanying the Panel Regulations requires an annual report on the work of the panel for the year ending 31 March to be available by 30 June. The reports have to be made available to the local authority's social services committee, the Family Court Business Committee and the Department of Health. The Department received reports for 1991/92 from 55 of the 56 guardian panels. The format, length and degree of detail of the reports varied very considerably from panel to panel but typically they included elements required by the guidance namely:—

      a summary of activity of the panel members
      the breakdown of financial expenditure
      membership of the panel committee
      membership of the panel
      training activities
      key policy and practice developments
      priorities to be addressed in the period covered by the next report.

8.27   The reports provide an interesting and valuable insight into the work of the service. Consideration is being given to introducing a more uniform format and agreed technical definitions in future years. This would make comparison of the reports easier. It would facilitate the identification of areas of concerns and trends in the service. An overview of the reports has been prepared by the Department of Health and will shortly be distributed to panels, local authorities and Family Court Business Committees.

Meetings for Panel Managers

8.28   Despite the valuable, supportive role played by panel committees, panel managers work in relative isolation without the support of the hierarchical structure which normally exists in local authorities. The Social Services Inspectorate has organised regional meetings to provide support to panel managers. The priorities for such events are to identify and disseminate elements of good practice, to share mutual concerns and to devise methods of effective inter panel cooperation. In some areas there was a history of such meetings but in others they were an innovation. These meetings have also afforded the Department the opportunity to identify any areas of difficulty and to consider what action if any the Department could take to help to resolve matters.

8.29   In addition a one day national conference for panel managers took place on 14 January 1993 with key note speakers from the Department and the Judiciary. The conference followed up and built on the first national conference held in July 1991. Subsequent sessions took the form of workshops. The topics addressed had been chosen by panel managers as the ones of most concern to them. A full report of the day's proceedings is due to be published at the end of January. The meeting acted as a useful contact between the Department and guardian panels enabling an exchange of information to take place and an up-to-date assessment to be made of the state of the service throughout the country. Amongst the issues raised in the meeting were the difficulties which arise from the wide varieties in pay and conditions of guardians around the country. Concern was also expressed about the very substantial legal fees which could be charged where guardians have to have separate legal representation in cases, especially if these go to appeal.

Court Committees

8.30   The Family Court Committee network established by the Lord Chancellor's Department also has a valuable role to play in monitoring the panel guardian service. Any difficulties which are being experienced with the service can be raised in these fora. So far as the Family Court Business Committees are concerned the panel manager acts as the focus and contact for guardians. In the case of the Family Court Service Committees guardians are appointed to the core membership. The panel guardian service is making a useful contribution to both these fora and and the manager of the Inner and North London Panel is also a member the Central Children Act Advisory Committee.

General

8.31   Overall the GALRO service appears to be performing well. A more dedicated work force is in place than previously. There are sufficient guardians on panels to undertake work promptly, eliminating the delays that bedevilled the service in some parts of the country before October 1991. The service provided to both Family Proceedings Courts and the higher courts appears to be effective and to be working well.

8.32   It is vital to ensure that the guardian work force continues to be well trained and keeps their knowledge up to date for the tasks they have to undertake. The courses which are being organised by the National Association have a valuable role to play in achieving this. Good practice also needs to be identified and disseminated. The regular meetings of panel managers around the country provide an excellent opportunity for exchanging information and for panel managers to learn from one another. It is important that these meetings should continue to take place regularly in all parts of the country.

Chapter 9: Review of Training in the Child Care Field

Background

9.1 Under Section 83 of the Children Act 1989 the Secretary of State for Health has a duty to keep under review the adequacy of the provision of child care training. This Chapter fulfils that requirement. It takes account of representations received for the purpose from the Central Council for Education and Training in Social Work (CCETSW), the Association of County Councils (ACC), the Association of Metropolitan Authorities (AMA), the Association of Directors of Social Services (ADSS), the National Council of Voluntary Child Care Organisations and other leading voluntary organisations in the child care field.

9.2 Views were sought as to whether the quantity and quality of social work training available at all levels—vocational, pre-qualifying, qualifying and post-qualifying is sufficient to meet the needs of those working in children's services. Organisations were asked to comment on perceived inadequacies and to identify groups of child care staff most affected.

9.3 The following common themes emerged from the responses:

- Successful implementation of the Children Act requires more than a strategy to train the field staff of social welfare agencies. There are whole areas of practice within Social Services responsibilities, for example through family centre workers, family aides, child minders, foster carers etc whose training needs have so far been inadequately met.

- A three year training course is essential if social workers are to acquire the necessary skills and knowledge to work in complex child care situations.

- The training needs of residential child care staff are particularly great and need to be given high priority.

- Investment is needed to develop and deliver a fully coherent National Vocational Qualification framework for training, assessment and profession of employers at pre-qualifying levels.

- The cost of secondment to qualifying training for these staff already in post has affected the take-up of Dip SW places.

- There is a tension between post-qualifying training delivered in-house (which is highly cost-effective but usually lacks accreditation) and external courses (which are accredited but are more expensive for local authorities).

9.4 A considerable amount of additional information has also been provided about the levels of training undertaken and the areas of specialisation by staff and volunteers in a number of leading child care voluntary organisations. This has proved helpful and demonstrates a continuing and widespread commitment to training right across the board and at all levels.

Training Continuum

9.5 The training needs of workers in the child care field are addressed through the comprehensive system of education, training and qualifications which CCETSW is working to develop for all social work and care staff employed in the personal social services. The development of a training "continuum" has been fully supported by the Department of Health which has been working in partnership with CCETSW to improve the training available for social services staff. In 1991 the Department launched its Training Strategy for the Personal Social Services and announced a major new investment in PSS Training. Under the Training Strategy an additional £10.4 million was provided in 1991/92, rising to £19.6 million in 1993/94. These new resources will strengthen the training available for all social services staff, including those in child care.

9.6 While Government determines policy on training issues, the prime responsibility for ensuring that staff are appropriately trained for their jobs must rest with employers, whether in the statutory, voluntary or private sectors. The Department of Health has, however, taken steps to promote training by local authority employers, particularly through the Training Support Programme, its specific grant, the child care programme of which stood at £12.5 million in 1991/92. The TSP Child Care has done much to support and promote local authority training activity. Further details are given below.

National Vocational Qualifications

9.7   The structure of national vocational qualifications (NVQ) provides a new national framework for training and qualifications for staff in the child care field. CCETSW is working through the Joint Awarding Bodies to develop NVQs in the care sector as quickly as possible and the Child Care and Education Awards, covering work with children under 8 years of age, were accredited by the National Council for Vocational Qualifications in September 1991. The Awards in Care, developed for health and social services staff, also have relevance for child care workers. Both these sets of awards provide NVQs at levels II and III.

9.8   There are still some significant gaps in awards for work with children in the 8–18 year age range and also in level IV work with children. The Care Sector Consortium has agreed to remedy these deficiencies following the report of a feasibility study completed in October 1992.

9.9   As NVQ awards become available, employers will need to identify the level of skills needed by their staff engaged in child care work and determine whether vocational or professional qualifications are most appropriate. The Training Support programme already supports a significant amount of training leading to NVQs.

Diploma in Social Work

9.10   CCETSW is working to introduce the Diploma in Social Work as the unified professional qualification for all social workers in all settings, replacing the former Certificate of Qualification in Social Work and the Certificate in Social Studies. Ninety-five per cent of the planned Dip SW programmes should be in place by March 1993. All qualifying training courses are required to teach child care, child protection and relevant legislation, including the Children Act. CCETSW published detailed notes of guidance on the teaching of child care in the Diploma and on the teaching of social work law (which covered child care law) in April 1991.

9.11   As part of its Training Strategy, and in recognition of the shortfall of student places available to achieve the estimated 5,500 annual output needed for the UK as a whole, the Department has made funding available for an extra 250 student grants. The Department believes that an initial two years qualification, re-inforced by appropriate post-qualifying training and experience remains the right approach.

9.12   The shortage of practice placements in local authorities is particularly acute in child care. Discussions are currently taking place between the Department, the Local Authority Associations, ADSS and CCETSW to explore possible ways forward in the light of the findings of the survey of placements published in June.

Post-Qualifying Training

9.13   Post-qualifying training is of great importance in providing practitioners, in the child care field as in other areas of social work, with additional knowledge and skills. CCETSW is working to introduce a new post-qualifying framework managed by regional consortia of education and employment interests and offering for the first time opportunities for large numbers of social workers to undertake further training. CCETSW staff are now working on competences for post-qualifying and advanced awards in child care. At present there are 15 CCETSW approved post-qualifying programmes in child care/child protection, with an intake of 162 students.

Quality Assurance

9.14   The Department of Health shares CCETSWs commitment to ensuring that all parts of the continuum achieve consistently high training standards. CCETSW achieves this through its approval and monitoring mechanisms which are set out in the published requirements for each stage of the training continuum. CCETSW plans to publish a handbook on Quality Assurance specifying the exact procedures for each level of the continuum.

Training Support Programme

9.15   The Government's Training Support Programme (TSP) began in 1988/89 as a specific grant of £7 million targeted at certain local authority staff working with elderly people. It was extended in value in 1989/90 to include staff working with children and their families. In 1990/91, £2.5 million grant was added specifically in respect of training for implementation of the Children Act and £2 million was provided to boost management training. Total grant was increased in 1991/92 to £12.5 million, including £3 million earmarked for Children Act training.

9.16   Each local authority has a responsibility to provide resources for the appropriate training of staff working in all areas of service delivery. The Training Support Programme is intended to supplement these. It aims to improve both the quality of social services provision and the management of those services by encouraging authorities to improve their training infrastructure, by targeting resources, and by generally increasing the availability of training. Authorities were also encouraged to invite foster parents and staff of NHS, private and voluntary sectors involved in providing care for children to their training courses and training events.

9.17   The Training Support Programme is widely valued for the assistance it provides to local authority training activity. It has given an important boost to the training available for all levels of the social services workforce and, as such, is a key component of the Department's Training strategy.

9.18   A summary of Local Authority targets and achievements under TSP Child Care for the years 1990/91 to 1992/93 is presented in Table 9.1 at the end of this chapter. This shows that for 1991/92 (the final year in which separate Children Act training data was collected) almost 79,000 course attendances on Children Act training were funded by the programme—49% of all course attendances. In that year local authorities planned to spend £21.9 million on all Child Care/Children Act training. The programme also supported a number of centrally organised initiatives including:

(i)   A project to provide training and support for key managers, training organisers and trainers responsible for implementing the Children Act;

(ii)   Publication and distribution of a Children Act news-sheet, "Implementation News", followed by "Children Act News" to promote the exchange and dissemination of practice and training issues arising from the implementation of the Children Act;

(iii) The commissioning and dissemination of a variety of Children Act training materials including a manual for guardians *ad litem*and reporting officers (see Annex C); and

(iv)   The development of Child Sex Abuse guidelines.

9.19   TSP Child Care has been increased again in 1992/93 to £14.5 million grant and contains within it a new initiative, known as the Residential Child Care Initiative as part of Government's response to the Utting Report "Children in the Public Care".

9.20   The Social Services Inspectorate carried out inspections of four social services departments to assess the impact of training carried out under the aegis of the Training Support Programme (Child Care) on child care and child protection practice. The inspection team judged that the progress achieved in the space of 18 months (since the introduction of the Programme) has been considerable, and served to reinforce the wisdom of extending specific grant funding for subsequent years. In particular:

●   the TSP Child Care initiative had enabled the four social services departments to expand and improve training opportunities for staff in field, residential and day care settings;

●   the training was highly valued by those who had undertaken it and managers at all levels were convinced that it had improved the confidence and competence of their staff.

9.21   However, the impact of the programme could have been enhanced in each local authority if:

- the development of the training plan and subsequent programme of courses and events had been a more participative process and "owned" by the whole organisation;

- more training had been provided for managers and supervisors, thus increasing the likelihood of the impact of training on practice being reinforced by effective supervision;

- the TSP had been integrated into the strategic thrust of each social services departments policies for both services and human resource development.

A report, which included a number of key recommendations, was produced and widely circulated.

Wales

9.22   The Training Support Programme in Wales has provided targeted funds, by means of specific grants, for child care training for social services staff since 1988/89. Additional funding for implementation of the Children Act 1989 was introduced in 1990/91, continuing in 1991/92 and 1992/93. Increasingly social services departments have sought to include staff from other agencies in aspects of child care training, particularly that concerned with child protection and implementation of the Children Act. All counties have child care training strategies designed to equip staff to provide services which meet the requirements and philosophy of the Children Act. In 1991/92 the Training Support Programme supported expenditure of some £900,000 on child care and Children Act training, from which social services departments provided Children Act training to over 3,500 of their own staff and over 1,500 staff from other agencies, and child care training to nearly 3,000 social services staff, and over 1,000 staff from other agencies. This year grant assistance of £635,000 has been given to support expenditure of £907,000 on child care and Children Act training.

Residential Child Care

9.23   Sir William Utting's 1991 review "Children in the Public Care" identified that 70% of all care staff in local authority homes were unqualified and recommended that all heads of homes and a proportion of care staff, perhaps up to one-third, should hold the Diploma in Social Work.

9.24   In response, the Department of Health launched in 1991 a Residential Child Care Initiative, using £1.7 million from the 1992/93 Training Support Programme. The aim of the Initiative is to increase the level of qualification among heads and deputy heads of homes. Eight Dip SW programmes were identified and helped to establish areas of particular practice in residential child care. The Initiative has been broadly welcomed by local authorities and 144 senior staff from homes are due to begin training in 1992/93. Twelve of these staff are from voluntary organisations.

9.25   CCETSW has also convened an Expert Group to draw up guidance on the content of qualifying training for residential child care workers. The Group's report, together with a more specific CCETSW guidance document on the knowledge, skills and competences needed for work in residential child care, was published in Autumn 1992 and circulated to all Diploma in Social Work Programmes.

Child Protection Training

9.26   Considerable public interest has been expressed in the quality of child protection training. The Diploma in Social Work is designed to give students familiarity with all the main issues and CCETSW's Notes of Guidance cover the area of child protection. CCETSW has expressed the view that it is not possible in a two year qualification to bring students to a level which would enable them to take key worker responsibilities in child protection immediately on qualifying. CCETSW takes the view that the first two years after qualification should be regarded as the period in which the social worker gains substantial further competence in child protection. ADSS and ACC believe that staff should have two years post-qualifying experience before they take the key worker role in child protection cases, while recognising that this is not at present possible in practice.

9.27 It is essential that social workers have sufficient knowledge and experience to be able to carry out complex and sensitive child protection work effectively. Discussions with CCETSW, ADSS and the Local Authority Associations are continuing around these issues.

Training Needs of the Voluntary Sector

9.28 Voluntary child care organisations have expressed their view that more resources are needed for training in the voluntary sector. Small organisations in particular have problems releasing staff and finding resources for training. The Department has met representatives of the voluntary sector to explore possible ways of addressing the problem, without undermining the fundamental responsibility of employers to meet the training needs of their staff. Local authorities are already encouraged to involve voluntary organisation staff in training events organised under the Training Support Programme and the numbers of course attendances by staff from the voluntary sector on local authority sponsored courses has been increasing significantly, year on year. A further meeting between the Department and the voluntary sector has been arranged for early 1993.

9.29 The Children Act promotes the concept of a mixed economy of services provision. In order to encourage this and facilitate local authority provision by voluntary organisations a £250,000 training grant was made available to the voluntary sector in 1991/92. The grant, administered by the National Council for Voluntary Child Care Organisations on behalf of the Department of Health, was allocated among 76 different voluntary agencies in accordance with agreed criteria.

9.30 An audited report prepared by the NCVCCO highlighted the diverse range of training which occurred as a result of the initiative. In total 7,886 people were trained at a cost of £31.98 per head. The amount of grant received by individual organisations ranged from £80 to £50,500 and the numbers of staff/volunteers trained varied from 2 to 1,200 across the wide span of child care services. The report acknowledged a greater level of awareness in the voluntary sector of issues around Children Act implementation as a result of the initiative and of improved practices, joint training and increased consultation with local authorities. The report was of the opinion, however, that a range of training needs still exists and that given the complexity of the Children Act there remains a need for more resources for training.

9.31 Ministers take the view that staff training in the voluntary sector should remain a management and financial responsibility of voluntary bodies. However, they will be willing to make some further financial support available of £200,000 in 1993–94, £250,000 in 1994–95 and £300,000 in 1995–96 as a temporary contribution to give concrete help to bodies lacking the infrastructure necessary to take advantage of the training opportunities available. The availability of this finance will be dependent on suitable proposals coming forward from voluntary interests.

9.32 In Wales grants totalling £30,196 were awarded to 7 voluntary organisations to assist also in training personnel and volunteers on Children Act implementation. The grants were made under the "Support for Child and Family Services" grant scheme.

General

9.33 The Department will continue to monitor the adequacy of child care training in order to ensure that the training needs of workers in the child care field are fully addressed through the social services training continuum. Government will work in partnership with CCETSW to strengthen training opportunities for all social services staff and will seek to update its own training strategy to take account of changing needs and priorities. A key task in 1993 will be implementing the recommendations of the policy review of CCETSW. The Department of Health will also continue to engage with the Local Authority Associations, ADSS, CCETSW and key voluntary bodies on issues of importance, such as training for child protection work and the training needs of the voluntary sector.

TABLE 9.1   Training Support Programme

Child Care/Children Act Sub-Programme (including Management Development and Post Qualifying training)—Financial Year 1991/92

Summary of Targets and Achievements over Three Years

	TSP 1990/91		TSP 1991/92		TSP 1992/93	
	Target	Achieve-ment	Target	Achieve-ment	Target	Achieve-ment
1. Training Achievements	No.	No.	No.	No.	No.	No.
Course Attendances						
2.1 Basic skills/Background	62,256	61,314	26,370	32,666	50,252	—
2.2 Vocational Training	—	—	2,913	2,609	9,002	—
2.3 Other – Non Qualifying	—	—	31,317	28,643	48,204	—
2.4 DipSW/CQSW/CSS	850	1,165	915	898	996	—
2.5 Post Qualifying	—	—	3,099	4,380	4,401	—
2.6 Management Development	13,458	12,931	7,468	7,014	8,638	—
2.7 Children Act	59,427	53,776	69,117	78,922	n/a	—
2.8 Total course attendances	135,991	129,186	141,199	155,132	121,493	n/a
2. Training Staff/Support Staff (WTE)	263.2	276.6	326.1	266.1	345.1	n/a
3. Additional Practice Placement Days provided	3,383	11,568	10,948	16,129	19,313	n/a
4. Training provided to staff of:						
4.1 NHS	—	9,942	—	10,302	—	—
4.2 Private Sector	—	975	—	669	—	—
4.3 Voluntary Sector	—	2,911	—	2,979	—	—
4.4 Others – Police, Teachers, etc.	—		—	13,936	—	—
4.5 Total	—	13,828	—	27,886	—	
5. Grant Details:						
5.1 Total Grant Provided (including top-slice)	£10.8 million		£12.5 million		£14.5 million	
5.2 Expenditure Supported (Planned)	£18.5 million		£21.9 million		£24.8 million	

PART III

Chapter 10: Issues and Work in Progress

Summary of Progress

10.1   After just one year of the Children Act in operation it would be premature to make any kind of judgement on the overall impact of the Act on children's services.

10.2   There are nevertheless a number of indications that the intentions of Parliament as expressed in the Act are beginning to be realised. Preliminary findings from this report which provide hopeful pointers towards successful implementation are the following:

> (1) In the period 31 March 1991 to 31 March 1992 there was a drop in numbers of some 5,000 in England who were being looked after by local authorities. *This indicates progress towards meeting major principles embedded in the Act : that children are generally best looked after within the family; and that parents experiencing difficulties should be offered help to keep the children within their family.*

> (2) There has been a reduction in the numbers of public law applications to protect children through emergency protection orders or care orders. *This fulfils the principle that action to protect children should take the least coercive course consistent with the interests of the welfare of children.*

> (3) At 31 March 1992 the statistical returns revealed that after 6 months of the Act, there was a shift in the proportion of those children looked after through voluntary arrangements (compared with those looked after under a court order). *There are indications that this has been achieved in part through new initiatives by social workers working in co-operation with parents, as the Act intended.*

> (4) All authorities have now established systems to receive representations and complaints about services from children who use the services, from their parents and from those who care for them.

> (5) All authorities have now established properly managed panels of Guardians *ad litem* and Reporting Officers to fulfil the new requirements of the Act. This process was assisted by the means of a targeted direct Government grant which could not be claimed by authorities until essential management criteria were met. GALRO panel managers are now generally able to offer courts the names of available Guardians *ad litem* for early appointment, whereas prior to implementation there had been mounting concern about delays.

> (6) Local authorities are generally to be congratulated on their vigorous response to their important new duties to safeguard and promote the welfare of children accommodated in independent schools. Amongst these schools are those who provide for children with special needs.

> (7) Many authorities have gone to considerable lengths to publicise their services and bring them to the notice of those in particular who may need them. This includes publishing information in a variety of languages according to the communities served and presenting information which is accessible to people with sensory disabilities.

10.3   There are, however, a number of areas where progress one year on was less advanced.

> (1) Slow progress to re-register existing independent (private and voluntary) day care services for under 8s against new Regulations was a cause for concern. Failure to re-register these services after 12 months leave the providers vulnerable to operating unlawfully, generally through no fault of their own. Local authorities will need to look to their registration systems to ensure that new registrations are dealt with promptly.

(2) Similarly slowness of authorities to inspect and register the services of those who apply to register private children's homes (a new requirement) was a cause for concern. Applications for registration which were not processed 12 months after application are deemed under the Act to have been refused; if this is due to inaction of the authority, rather than unsuitability of the children's home then this is of considerable concern.

(3) Since before the Act was implemented there had been concern about known child protection cases which were not allocated to a social worker. The number of unallocated cases has declined slightly overall. Some authorities have demonstrated that they were able to take vigorous action to make dramatic improvements; others have been less energetic and less successful. *The basic requirements of the Act cannot be fulfilled in respect of unallocated cases.*

(4) In some areas there was slow or incomplete progress in authorities seeking out the extent of children in need in their areas and developing services to meet them. This is a matter of considerable concern because the insufficiency of family support services could lead to the avoidable use of coercive intervention through the courts. This would not be consistent with the intentions of the Act.

(5) There is concern too that authorities may not have pursued with sufficient vigour opportunities to develop services with voluntary bodies and independent agencies.

10.4 For the first time, with the Act, authorities have an extensive range of Regulations and guidance, providing clear statements of standards in most areas of child care services. Many of the areas of concern mentioned above have been long-standing issues which are thrown into sharp relief by these newly articulated standards in ways which previously would have been more difficult to discern.

Roles of JAFIG and JUIG

10.5 With the launch of its monitoring strategy the Department of Health paved the way for a rigorous scrutiny of the Children Act implementation process. Early difficulties identified in this report will continue to be monitored closely by a variety of means. The roles of JAFIG and JUIG as fora for dialogue between Government departments, local authority, voluntary and training interests on Children Act issues in general and residential care in particular have already been discussed.

SSI Work Programme

10.6 SSI will continue its comprehensive programme of child care policy and development work alongside a series of small scale inspections. Areas of development work targeted for next year include:—

● promotion and dissemination of guidance on private fostering

● assessing outcomes for children looked after

● review of staff ratios for under 8s and local child care plans

● family support services

● GALRO and court welfare services generally

● review of the work of Area Child Protection Committees and monitoring implementation of Working Together, including unallocated cases

● residential care issues arising from JUIG and the Warner report.

10.7 The provisions of the Act covered by the inspection programme is equally wideranging and will cover residential child care including voluntary children's homes, secure accommodation, education of children looked after, children in need including children with disabilities, child protection services, private fostering, juvenile justice and the GALRO service.

Child Care Research Programme

10.8   Research too has a pivotal role to play in monitoring and ultimately evaluating the impact of the Children Act. Twelve studies have so far been commissioned to investigate and evaluate aspects of the early working of the Act. (For project details see annex 1). In addition to these studies (which have a specific Children Act focus) there is also an extensive programme of research covering all aspects of services to children encompassed by the Children Act.

Child Protection and the Courts

10.9   Two research studies have been commissioned to look at new provisions concerning child protection. The first will consider a pre-court stage in which the child's personal and family circumstances are assessed by the local authority. It will investigate the process by which cases are handled by the local authority in stages leading up to possible court intervention, focusing on the determination of a child at risk of "significant harm" (project 1).

10.10   A second study 'Statutory Intervention Under the Children Act' will look at compulsory intervention in cases of child protection and its management by the courts. In particular this study will look at how the new extended menu of orders is used by the courts (project 2).

Family Support and Services to Children in Need

10.11   Four major studies are underway to look at how local authorities are responding to the challenge introduced by the Act to extend and improve the provision of family support services to children in need. First is a study directed by Jean Packman at Bristol University. This study, whose start date coincided with implementation of the Act, will trace the translation of policy into practice in two local authorities and examine the effect on families in terms of services offered (project 3).

10.12   A second study 'The Use of Short Term Accommodation Under the Children Act' led by Jane Aldgate at Barnett House, Oxford, will focus on innovative examples of good practice. Taking a sample of respite care schemes drawn from two local authorities which have taken an early lead in establishing new services, the study which traces the progress of users of the schemes will also evaluate the impact of services provided on families and children (project 4).

10.13   To meet the duty to promote the upbringing of children in need, local authorities are required to identify children in need in their areas. A linked study conducted jointly with Jane Tunstill of NVCCO will look at how need is defined by Local Authorities and at how policies are being developed in relation to children in need in their area (project 5).

10.14   An important group brought newly within the framework of children's legislation under the Act are children with disabilities. A study on The Effect of Services to Children with Disabilities will examine ways in which local authorities are interpreting their new responsibilities to disabled children and identify and promote areas of good practice. An important aim of the study is to develop tools for use by practitioners (project 6).

Daycare and Under Eights

10.15   Two important studies have been commissioned from the Thomas Coram Research Unit in connection with services to children under eight. The first by Pat Petrie, commissioned before the Act was implemented, aims to characterise and classify day care services for school age children subject to regulation under the Act and to develop an understanding of the factors which contribute to the successful meeting of goals (project 8).

10.16   The second study, conducted by Peter Moss and Charlie Owen, will trace the actions undertaken in 18 Local Authorities to implement the new provisions (project 7). A parallel study is being undertaken in Wales. It adopts a broadly similar approach to the English study but pays added attention to implementing the Act's provisions in rural areas and to the issue of the Welsh language.

Review Duty

10.17 The Children Act strengthens the duty on local authorities concerning the planning and review of children's cases by requiring that children looked after are the subject of a statutory review at least every six months. A recently commissioned study to be led by Ruth Sinclair at National Children's Bureau will compare how the new arrangements for planning and review are being operated against those in place pre-Act (project 9).

Residential Care

10.18 Under the Act, inspection of local authority and private homes will be undertaken by 'arms length' inspection units. A research study has recently been commissioned at York University to inform the inspection process. The study: the 'Role and Quality of Residential Care' will focus on the structural factors such as size, mix of children and on process factors such are care plans and staff practice which appear to lead to good outcomes and hence draw out implications for external management and quality assurance (project 10).

Leaving Care

10.19 The statutory requirement on local authorities to prepare all the children they are looking after for the time they leave care is a new duty, introduced under the Act although it did no more than reinforce what had already been good practice in many settings. A recently completed study on Return Home as experienced by Children in Care by the Dartington Research Unit has produced a valuable tool as an aid to practice concerning the issues which should be considered when preparing a child for leaving care. A second study commissioned before implementation will focus on good practice. The study being directed by Mike Stein at Leeds University will evaluate the impact of a small sample of innovatory leaving care schemes on young people and explore how the schemes are experienced by them (project 11).

The Guardian ad litem and Reporting Officer Service

10.20 Guardians *ad litem* are social workers appointed by courts in family proceedings. Their role is to advise the court on what is in the interests of the child and to ensure that the best wishes and feelings of the child are made clear to the court. In this capacity GALs may appoint expert witnesses on behalf of children to undertake assessments and advise the court on the child's behalf. A recently commissioned study, 'Guardians ad Litem—Expert Evidence and Child Care Proceedings' will investigate the policy and practice of guardians *ad litem* with the regard to the use of expert witnesses (project 12).

Centrally Commissioned Training Materials

10.21 Through the Training Support Programme the Department is continuing to commission and disseminate a variety of Children Act related training materials. These include:

- a two year project undertaken by Leeds University to produce leaving care materials for social services staff on the aftercare provisions of the Act;

- dissemination of new materials relating to children living outside their culture;

- the NCB Early Childhood Unit have been commissioned to produce four additional documents on race, culture, language and religion and Part X of the Children Act as part of their training pack;

- the National Childminders' Association are to develop and produce training materials to support childminders;

- the Family Rights Group have been funded to update their 'Working in Partnership with Families' Pack and to produce a supplementary stand-alone reader;

- the production of an accessible reference volume for new and experienced GALROs aimed specifically at the court craft element of the GALRO duties;

- the University of Bristol has been commissioned to develop training materials to assist social workers in the implementation of Outcome Measures in Child Care;

- the commissioning of training materials designed to assist residential care staff working with difficult adolescents is also under consideration.

Child Care Initiatives

10.22   In response to specific concerns around particular child care themes the Department of Health has launched the following series of initiatives, all of which can be expected to provide useful sources of information on progress in implementing the Children Act:

- The Department is spending £1.5 million over 3 years to pump prime expansion of day care for school age children. Twelve projects are being funded involving development officers working in different parts of the country to facilitate the expansion of services. Support is also being given to the central administration of Kids' Clubs Network, which is helping to support all the projects. A Small Grants Scheme, similar to the one run for under 5s services for the last six years, has also been set up. A total of £100,000 has been allocated for use as small grants in the first year;

- Another £1.5 million is being spent over 3 years on the Family Support Initiative to assist the development of services for children in need within their families. Grants are being made to 8 projects which include the production of training materials, advocacy, advice and counselling, information services and the promotion of inter-agency services.

- A child abuse treatment initiative was launched in 1990/91. The first stage of the initiative was the National Children's Home survey of existing treatment facilities for abused children and young perpetrators. The Department is currently making grants to support a number of projects by voluntary organisations providing different types and ranges of treatment.

- A child abuse training initiative was launched in 1986. Almost £3 million has been awarded since the initiative began.

- £3 million has been made available over 3 years to support the single homeless young people initiative. This initiative was introduced in 1991 in response to concerns about the numbers of young people sleeping rough in London and that care leavers and, in particular, those leaving residential care formed a significant proportion of them.

UN Convention

10.23   Finally, implementation of the Children Act with respect to the rights of the child will be monitored closely as part of the Department of Health's wider responsibility for co-ordinating action on progress in implementing the UN Convention. Having ratified the Convention the UK Government is required to report to the Committee on the Rights of the Child by 14 January 1994 on progress made in giving effect to those rights. Part of this task will be to establish whether there are any areas of potential difficulty where UK legislation, policy or practice may not fully coincide with the principles of the Convention.

ANNEXES

ANNEX A

**DEPARTMENT OF HEALTH
CHILD CARE RESEARCH PROGRAMME**

Portfolio of Abstracts of Current Research

Project 1: The Implementation of the 1989 Children Act in Respect of Children in Need of Protection

Date started:	October 1992
Completion date:	September 1995
Research director/s:	Dr June Thoburn
Project address:	University of East Anglia Social Work Development Unit Norwich NR4 7TJ
Telephone no:	0603 56161 x2057

Research Abstract:

The study will focus on the impact of the 1989 Children Act on services for children in need of protection. The Act requires local authorities to "take reasonable steps through the provision of services under Part III of this Act to prevent children within their area suffering ill-treatment or neglect", and to reduce the need to bring proceedings for care or supervision orders. There will be approximately 35 children in each group, from two or three local authorities, one of which will include a substantial number of black children. The study will be essentially descriptive and use qualitative methods. The outcome for the children 12 months after the conference will be considered in the light of a range of variables, including the method of intervention, and the use or otherwise of compulsory measures.

Project 2: Statutory Intervention in Child Care; The Impact of the Children Act

Date started:	June 1991
Completion date:	December 1994
Research director/s:	Ms J Hunt Ms A McLeod
Project address:	University of Bristol 22 Berkeley Square Bristol BS8 IHP
Telephone no:	0272 303030

Research Abstract:

This study will look at compulsory intervention in cases of child protection and its management by the courts. It will trace a cohort of cases to chronicle the process by which court orders are sought or not. It will focus particularly on 2 aspects of change, namely: the extended menu of orders; the principle that delay is regarded as detrimental. The findings will be set against a baseline drawn from earlier research.

Project 3: Accommodation: The Implementation of Section 20 of the Children Act 1989

Date Started:	October 1991
Completion Date:	September 1994
Research director/s:	Dr Jean Packman
Project Address:	Dartington Research Unit Fox Hole Dartington Totnes Devon TQ9 6EB
Telephone:	0803 862231

Research Abstract:

The aim of the study is to investigate the implementation of Section 20 of the Children Act 1989 to determine the extent and nature of changing policy and practice. It has three main foci. Firstly to compare policy and practice before and after the Act using a previous study as a baseline. Secondly to examine the effects of implementation of policies on 'accommodation' under the Act including looking at the range of problems addressed, the type of accommodation and length of stay; and thirdly to look at formal and informal processes of negotiation about the need for 'accommodation' between parents, children and social services staff.

Project 4: The Use of Short Term Accommodation Under the Children Act 1989

Date started:	April 1991
Completion date:	June 1995
Research director/s:	Dr Jane Aldgate
Project address:	University of Oxford
	Dept of Applied Social Studies
	Barnett House
	Wellington Square
	Oxford OXI 2ER
Telephone no:	0865 270325

Research Abstract:

This is a two part study involving a nationwide and intensive investigation of the use of respite accommodation under the Children Act 1989. The aim of the first part, is to undertake concurrently with the intensive study, a mapping exercise. It will involve a survey of existing practice and plans for change.

The intensive study is designed as a before and after study. It is a three year study in two local authorities. At the beginning of the intervention there will be an investigation of the characteristics of users and the purpose of accommodation seen from the perspective of clients, carers and social workers and the extent of consultation and partnership arrangements. After the intervention the outcome of using respite accommodation over time will be investigated to identify factors contributing to its success or failure. Data collection will be by interview and standardised research instruments. A primary aim is that the results of the study and some of its methodology can be used directly to enhance social work practice.

Project 5: Children in Need Study

Date started:	July 1992
Completion date:	August 1993
Research director/s:	Dr Jane Aldgate
Project address:	University of Oxford
	Barnett House
	Wellington Street
	Oxford OXI 2ER
Telephone no:	0865 270325

Research Abstract:

The aim of this study is to provide an overview of how local authorities in England are responding to the requirements in the Children Act 1989 in relation to the definition and implementation of policies and practices for children in need. Data collection will be by postal questionnaire and telephone interviews to establish: how authorities define children in need and priority service provision within this definition; how authorities are allocating resources for family support services; identifying what arrangements authorities are adopting to implement a corporate approach; and to investigate the implementation of consultation processes and the publishing of services.

Project 6: Effect of the Children Act on Services to Disabled Children

Date started:	August 1991
Completion date:	December 1994
Research director/s:	Ms C Robinson
Project address:	University of Bristol
	22 Berkeley Square
	Bristol BS8 1HP
Telephone no:	0272 303030

Research Abstract:

The overall objective of the study is to examine the ways in which local authorities are interpreting their new responsibilities towards disabled children under the Children Act and to identify and promote areas of good practice. The aims are to obtain a national overview of local authorities response to their new responsibilities, to conduct "process evaluations" of 3 children's and teenagers' services in each of six local authority areas and finally to hold a conference to disseminate the findings.

Project 7: A Study of Local Authority Implementation of the Provisions of the Children Act on Day Care and Pre-school Education

Date started:	May 1992
Completion date:	December 1995
Research director/s:	Professor McGurk
Project address:	Thomas Coram Research Unit
	27-28 Woburn Square
	London WCIH 0AA
Telephone no:	612 6957

Research Abstract:

This project will monitor the implementation by English local authorities of the provisions of the Children Act on day care services for children under 8 and pre-school education, and evaluate the impact of that implementation. It will also consider the effects of certain organisational differences between local authorities, including the use of Independent Inspection units for implementation of parts of the Act and the transfer of responsibility of all under 8s services to local education authorities. The project would involve two visits to a stratified random sample of 18 English local authorities, the first focusing on implementation of the Act, the second focusing on evaluation of the Act. During these visits, interviews will be conducted with a range of policy makers, managers, practitioners and representatives of organisations. In five of the local authorities a sample of users of the services will be interviewed. These interviews will be supplemented by analysis of documents prepared by each local authority in the sample. Results would be reported back to local authorities through conferences and publications during the course of the project.

Project 8: Out of Schools Services

Date started:	October 1990
Completion date:	December 1993
Research director/s:	Dr Pat Petrie
Project address:	Thomas Coram Research Unit
	Institute of Education
	41 Brunswick Square
	London WCI IAZ
Telephone no:	636 1500

Research Abstract:

Daycare services and supervised activities attended by school age children outside school hours and in the holidays are brought into the regulation of local authorities under the Children Act 1989.

The aim of this project is to characterise and classify daycare services for school age children subject to regulation under the Children Act 1989. It is based on 12 case studies and a survey of 100 play/care schemes.

Provision will be described on the basis of major values, goals and the aspects of organisation of these services. The aim will be to develop an understanding of the factors which contribute towards the successful meeting of goals or failure to do so and to identify indicators of this. The final aim is to develop a basis for monitoring and evaluation.

Project 9: Planning and Reviewing Cases Under the Children Act 1989

Date started:	January 1993
Completion date:	December 1995
Research director/s:	Dr Ruth Sinclair
Project address:	National Children's Bureau
	8 Wakley Street
	London ECIV 7QE
Telephone no:	278 9441

Research Abstract:

The aim of the study is to map the way in which local authorities have translated the 'Arrangements for Placement' and 'Review of Children's Cases' Regulations into practice. To examine in some detail the extent to which the operation of local planning and review systems complies with the regulations and furthers the underlying principles of the Children Act. To consider the contribution of the planning and review intervention with a child and his or her family. In addition to identifying ways in which the planning of individual cases can be aggregated to provide useful management information, including information on outcomes.

Project 10: The Role and Quality of Residential Care

Date started:	January 1993
Completion date:	December 1995
Research director/s:	Prof Ian Sinclair
Project address:	Univerity of York
	Heslington
	York YO1 5DD
Telephone no:	0904 430000

Research Abstract:

The project will focus on residential care for children and aim to, identify the structural factors (eg size, mix of children) and process factors (eg staff practices, care plans) which tend to produce "good outcomes", as well as draw implications for the definition of good quality care and hence for management, training and quality assurance.

Project 11: A Study of Leaving Care Schemes

Date started:	October 1990
Completion date:	September 1994
Research director/s:	Mr M Stein
Project address:	School of Cont Education
	Dept of External Studies
	University of Leeds
	Leeds LS2 9JT
Telephone no:	0532 333214

Research Abstract:

This project is undertaking a four-year study of leaving care schemes representative of the four main models of current provision: residential care; leaving care project; integrated care; and specialist care. It aims to identify policies and practices which are supportive to young people leaving care. The research focuses on a detailed account of each scheme, and a follow-up study of a representative sample of young people who join them, including a profile of their care histories, project careers—from both their own and their key workers' perspectives, and their transition from scheme support to their own living arrangements. Data are being gathered using interviews, personal documents, observation and group discussion, together with a literature review, case history profile, project reports and local comparative data on young people not in care in the selected areas.

Project 12: Guardians ad Litem, Expert Evidence and Child Care Proceedings

Date started:	October 1992
Completion date:	September 1996
Research director/s:	Dr J Brophy
Project address:	Thomas Coram Research Unit
	Institute of Education
	41 Brunswick Square
	London WC1 1AZ
Telephone no:	636 1500

Research Abstract:

This project will investigate the policy and practice of guardians *ad litem* with regard to the use of expert evidence in child care and related proceedings. It aims to examine attitudes towards, and use of child experts, the circumstances in which expert evidence is most commonly sought, the briefing practices adopted and the impact of such evidence in the work of guardians. The study will also examine the role of directions appointments in family proceedings courts as a mechanism for achieving the evidence.

CHILDREN ACT
RELATED GOVERNMENT REPORTS AND INQUIRIES 1992

- **Accommodating Children.** A review of children's homes in Wales by the Social Services Inspectorate of the Welsh Office, published January 1992.

- **The Quality of Care.** A report of the Residential Staff Inquiry chaired by Lady Howe, "To inquire into the pay, conditions of service, training and qualifications of residential staff employed in homes and hostels covered by the Residential and Allied Staffs Committee. Issues which had a bearing on the inquiry include:

  - Recruitment and retention;
  - Career development;
  - Management and organisational practice;
  - Status and responsibility;
  - Working patterns

  The report was published June 1992.

- **Ty Mawr Community Homes Inquiry.** Report of the Inquiry by Gareth Williams QC and Mr John McCreadie MED, "To inquire into the management and control of the Ty Mawr Community Home at Gilwern, in Gwent, having regard to allegations of mistreatment of children and young people there: to determine, on a full and fair view of the management regime and practical day to day running at Ty Mawr, whether allegations of a regime which encouraged, permitted or acquiesced in brutal or emotionally cruel treatment of children and young persons are well-founded; and to make recommendation in the interests of the children and young people who live there." Published in August 1992.

- **Children Act Advisory Committee Annual Report.** Chaired by Mrs Justice Booth, "To advise the Lord Chancellor, the Home Secretary, the Secretary of State for Health and the President of the Family Division on whether the guiding principles of the Children Act 1989 are being achieved and whether the court procedures and the guardian *ad litem* system are operating satisfactorily." Published November 1992.

- **Choosing with Care.** Report on the selection, development and management of staff in children's homes, chaired by Norman Warner, "To examine selection and recruitment methods and criteria for staff working in children's homes and recommend practicable improvements; to make such further examination as the Committee may consider justified of management and other issues relevant to the protection of children and young people and to the support and guidance of staff in such homes; and to report with recommendations to the Secretary of State for Health." Published December 1992.

- **Another kind of Home.** Report of a Review of Residential Child Care in Scotland, "To examine the current provision of residential child care and the quality of service provided. To examine in part questions of training, control and sanctions, children's rights and inspection. To make recommendations for training and service of high quality." Published December 1992

ANNEX C

**CHILDREN ACT
PUBLICATIONS**

I Regulations and Guidance

Name of publication	Date of Issue/ Launch	ISBN No. or Reference No.
An introduction to the Children Act 1989	November 1989	0 11 321254 2
Volume 1—Court Orders	March 1991	0 11 321371 9
Volume 2—Family Support, Day Care and Educational Provision for Young Children	March 1991	0 11 321372 7
Volume 3—Family Placements	April 1991	0 11 321375 1
Volume 4—Residential Care	July 1991	0 11 321430 8
Volume 5—Independent Schools	April 1991	0 11 321373 5
Volume 6—Children with Disabilities	September 1991	0 11 321452 9
Volume 7—Guardians *ad litem* and other Court Related Issues	October 1991	0 11 321471 5
Volume 8—Private Fostering and Miscellaneous	October 1991	0 11 321473 1
Volume 9—Adoption Issues	October 1991	0 11 321474 X
Volume 10—Index	December 1992	0 11 321538 X
Patterns and Outcomes in Child Placement	May 1991	0 11 321357 3
Working Together under the Children Act 1989: A guide to arrangements for Inter-Agency Co-operation for the Protection of Children from Abuse (New edition)	October 1991	0 11 321472 3
The Welfare of Children in Boarding Schools Practice Guide	October 1991	0 11 321477 4
Registration of Childminding and Day care: Using the Law to Improve Standards	October 1991	0 11 321469 3
Practice Guide for GALROs	July 1992	0 11 321495 2
Guidance for GALRO Panel Managers	July 1992	0 11 321505 3
Timetabling of Care Proceedings before the implementation of the Children Act 1989	February 1992	0 11 321487 1
The Care of Children—Principles and Practice in Regulations and Guidance	1989	0 11 321289 5
Looking After Children—Assessing Outcomes in Child Care	December 1991	0 11 321459 6
The Children Act 1989: What every Nurse, Health Visitor and Midwife needs to know	March 1992	COI/HSSH J1548NJ O/N 19207
An Introductory Guide to the NHS	September 1991	COI/HSSH J1403NJ O/N 16050
Child protection: Guidance for Senior Nurses, Health Visitors and Midwives (Second edition 1992)	1992	0 11 321501 0
Guidance on completion of statistical returns	Generally included with the relevant returns	—

II Training Materials

Name of publication	Date of Issue/ Launch	ISBN No. or Reference No.
National Children's Bureau Children and Group Day care, aimed principally at those responsible for registration and inspection in SSDs	16 May 1991 Launched by Minister of Health	Participant's pack 0 90 281766 3 Trainers' pack 0 90 281767 1
National Children's Bureau Child Protection Training Project designed principally for local authority staff in relation to court orders obtainable for the protection of children	1 May 1991 Launched by Minister of Health	0 90 281762 0
Family Rights Group Working in Partnership with Children and Families and Communities. It aims to give social workers and their managers a thorough knowledge of the inter-relationship of law and practice in relation to partnership and prevention	24 July 1991 Launched by P.S.S. Health	0 11 321447 2

III Training and Materials Centrally Commissioned

Name and Description of Pack and Preparing Body	Date of Launch	ISBN No. or Reference No.
Open University "Putting it into Practice" Deals with the overall philosophy of the Children Act prepared jointly Department of Health with LCD Principally for social workers, local authority lawyers and magistrates	23 January 1991 Launched by Minister of Health 29 January 1991 Launched by Lord Chancellor	0 74 924348 1 —
Additional material for Chairmen of Family Proceedings Courts	May 1991	—
Training pack for NHS Professionals	August 1992	0 11 321518 5
P558: The Children Act: Court Order Cards 1–23 in Braille	December 1991	—
Leicester University Children in Need and their Families: A New Approach. A guide to Part III of the Act for local authority managers	November 1990	0 9511996 1 7
Manual for Senior Managers of SSDs Deals with the philosophy of the Act and major changes it brings about	May 1991	—
The Children Act—An Advisors Guide (video)	July 1991	—
University of East Anglia Training materials on Parental and Older Child Involvement in Child Protection Work	September 1992	—
Parentline Map of the Act	June 1992	0 9519430 0 6

IV   Children Act Publicity—Leaflets etc

Name of publication	Date of Launch	ISBN No. or Reference No.
The Children Act and the Courts—A Guide for Parents	1991	CAG2
The Children Act and Local Authorities—A Guide for Parents	1991	CAG1
The Children Act and You—A Guide for Young People (leaflet)	1991	CAG3
The Children Act and the Courts—A Guide for Children and Young People	1992	CAG6
Getting Help from the Social Service—A Guide for Children and Young People	1992	CAG5
Living Away from Home Your Rights—A Guide for Children and Young People	1992	CAG7
Children Act and Day Care—A Guide to the Law	1991	CAG4
Family Rights Group		
Child Protection Procedures—What they mean for your family	July 1992	—
Stepfamily		
A Step in Both Directions? The Impact of the Children Act 1989 on Stepfamilies	February 1992	1873309066

Printed in the United Kingdom for HMSO
DD 5060648   2/93   C85   51/4078   65536   Ord 229304   02/26183

ISBB
3466